REVIEWS

Joy Comes in the Morning is an autobiography for every person who has been on the verge of giving up, for every person who wearily looked up at the mountain that would need to be climbed to see their precious dreams fulfilled. This book is about victory over the circumstances and the challenges of life through the power of faith and deep-rooted strength. It takes the reader on a spiritual and emotional journey through Professor Enoh Ukpong's life – a life that most people weren't aware she has lived. With Enoh's contagious joviality, love and trust in the Lord, it's easy for most to see her as effortlessly attaining success without any idea of what she's lived through – what she has survived. This story allows us to examine even the smallest blessings that should not be taken for granted, giving us the inspiration to always aim higher.

—Evelyn

Joy Comes in the Morning held me hostage. I was unable to put it down. This true story spoke of the hardships of one person and the ability to overcome, at a young age, and the working miracles of Jesus. How a child could have such faith is beyond most adult's understanding of the torment she suffered. A range of emotions filled me. Many children are abused by family members who are supposed to love them, but most are unable to be determined enough to survive. Amazing grace how sweet the Lord is for this author to have the resilience to overcome, the determination to

continue, the strength to walk on in life. Without forgiveness one cannot move forward in their spiritual journey.

I would unconditionally recommend this book as top shelf reading.

—Paula Torres, RN

This is a personal description of a life full of adversity and experiences that shaped a strong, perseverant individual. An honest account of true feelings from a woman who faces challenges "head on" and brings spirit and joy to each morning!

—Susan Provost, RN, MSN

This book is a "must read". Joy Comes in the Morning reveals a person's journey of life that transpired through their belief in the "Glory of God". Enoh utilized her power of prayer and with the Grace of God to transition from her home country to life in the United States. Through her hard work, self-sacrifice, education, and most of all deep faith in the power of God, she achieved her dream. Enoh, in her later years, provides positive blessings and inspiration to all those around her.

—Linda Esper, EdD, RN

Three words describe this book, endurance, patience and hardwork, or better described as discipline, drive and determination.

Enoh came into my life on March 27, 2014 when my husband was in the hospital recovering from bacterial pneumonia with a secondary infection of hospital acquired pneumonia. I was sitting at my husband's bedside when it was time for the nurses' rotation. Enoh, the nursing instructor, and Jason, a nursing student-in-training, came into my husband's room and introduced themselves. Enoh so graciously asked my husband if Jason could take care of him for the day. As she watched while Jason did his care, Enoh and I were visiting. I could tell right then she was a very special nurse. That was the day I will never forget because Enoh and I have kept in touch ever since and she has become a dear sister in Christ and my friend.

I'm so thankful she shared her life experiences through her book. I knew some of her life journey, but now it's more complete. God has certainly been with her each step of her life and she isn't afraid to give our dear heavenly Father the praise and glory for how He has protected her and guided her through her life from then until now.

I would highly recommend this book to inspire you to continue to endure and to have patience in whatever you are going through in your life. Hard work always pays off, especially when God is a part of it. One needs discipline, drive and determination to get through life and Enoh has certainly demonstrated this. Enjoy her life story!

—Lorna Johnson

This book:

1. Encourages people in similar situations not to be frightened, if someone was able to come out successfully, they can too.

2. Encourages people in the Nursing profession who are about to give up due to one or two bad experiences to know that it's worth it being a nurse and never to give up.

3. Will also help someone who aspires to be a nurse, to know what the profession entails and help to prepare for it.

4. Encourages people to commit their endeavors to God, because with God all things are possible.

5. This book is very inspirational. I'm glad I had the opportunity to read it.

Thank you Professor Ukpong. May this book go viral across continents.

—Mavis Amankwah,
Family Nurse Practitioner, MSN

JOY COMES
in the
MORNING

The Power of
Drive, Discipline
and
Determination

Dr. Enoh Ukpong

CONTENTS

ACKNOWLEDGEMENTS

First, I would like to give God the glory, for helping me over-come all things. The Lord has been with me all the way in my life's journey. God has been providing, protecting, directing, comforting, correcting, and forgiving me. I could not do with-out Him each day.

To my Mother, who, due to circumstances and the times, never set foot in school since that was how it was then for women, but she had the innate intelligence to drill into us the significance of education which has always been the backbone of success. She worked hard to put all her children in school and found the means for their payment. My Mother taught her children the reward of honesty, hard work, and not quit-ting when we are in a difficult situation or when we fail. If we did fail, she would sit us down to walk us through why we failed and what and how we would learn from our mistakes. Sometimes children lie to their parents to avoid punishment. For me, I had no reason to lie, as Mom never saw a reason to punish me. Instead, she talked to me and reasoned with me, even as a little child. My Mother had unconditional love, patience and tolerance to explain things to me without yelling or punishing me when I was young. This made me very close to my Mother until the end of her life. Mom was my best friend, confidant and the best Mother in the whole world. I love you forever Mom! I know you are in heaven and I will be there with you when it is my time.

To my family who has given me stability and contentment in life.

To Linda Esper, Ed. D, who took time out of her busy schedule to read my first draft and was my inspiration to publish this book.

To Kathleen Healy, PhD, who was my God sent editor that I stumbled into in a miraculous way.

To my wonderful husband, who has been very supportive of me.

To all my friends who contributed in some way to make this book a reality.

The title of this memoir comes from Psalm 30, verse 5 that says, "Weeping may endure for a night but joy cometh in the morning." King James version.

PREFACE

This is a true story of my life written as I remember it. The names of the people are real. I have been through so much in my life, and I wanted to share it with others to encourage them to not give up when things or life itself does not go the way we expect. I never imagined that life would turn me upside down and inside out, until it happened. In the process of this tumultuous life's journey, I learned to depend on God while growing up, even when I did not fully understand what that meant. The Lord was there for me and with me. I used to talk to Him about all I was going through each day.

The best part of my life's journey was coming to know the Lord. I used to go to church with my parents and with my brother when I was living with him. I talked to God and depended on Him for a long time without fully understanding, until I encountered the Lord in my Nursing School in Nigeria. There, I came to know the risen Lord and He changed my life forever. To God be the Glory, for He has provided all my needs and He has given me the platform in Nursing to help those in need in many ways. I take this responsibility seriously, always giving my very best in all I do each day.

ABOUT THE AUTHOR

Professor Enoh Ukpong, PhD, MSN, RN, formerly known as Enoh Samuel Utuk, was born in the little village of Afaha-Atai, Eket, in the former Eastern Nigeria, to Bella Assam and Samuel Utuk. She left her village for Gusau in Northern Nigeria to live with her brother when she was about seven years of age. She never went back to her village to live, except for occasional visits. Her brother sponsored her early education up to high (secondary) school. Professor Ukpong has been on her own since she graduated from high school. She earned her Registered Nursing license from Wusasa Hospital School of Nursing, in Zaria, and her Midwifery license from Ramat Specialist Hospital School of Midwifery (previously known as Queen Elizabeth Hospital), Umuahia, in Nigeria before coming to the United States of America in January 1979 as a foreign student, to continue her professional pursuits.

She started working as a Nurse's Aide while going to college full time. Professor Ukpong worked two jobs to support herself in college. She did not have any idea about student loans and financial aid until later on. By the time she learned about student loans, she had already established herself by working 2-3 jobs to maintain herself. As a result, she never had any student loan. Professor Ukpong passed her LPN (License Practical Nursing) exam in 1979 and worked as an LPN until March of 1981 when she passed the Massachusetts Nursing State Board Exam and earned her RN (Registered Nursing) Certificate. She earned a Bachelor's degree in Public Health in May of 1981 and a Master's degree in Nursing at Anna Maria College in Paxton, Massachusetts in May of 1984. Professor Ukpong earned her Ph.D. in Nursing from Columbia Pacific University in 1989.

She would always strive to fit her nursing schedule with her children's education schedule when they were younger. It was not easy, but she did it. Looking back, she is thankful that the Lord gave her the strength and His grace to pull through successfully without any regret.

Professor Ukpong is happily married with three grown children and three grandchildren, all living in Worcester, Massachusetts. She has been blessed by the Lord, this is why she is sharing her story with you. The main message in Professor Ukpong's story is, "ENDURANCE, PATIENCE AND HARDWORK" pays off in the end. Humanly speaking, it can be tough sometimes, but with God, nothing is impossible.

FOREWORD

I first met Dr. Enoh at a challenging time in my life. I had been admitted to the emergency room with an infection in my blood. I had already been in the hospital for more than 5 days.

I was staring out the door of my hospital room, watching people go by in the hall. At this point I was more scared than I had ever been in my life. This was the first time I had been admitted to the hospital since I was born. I was having all kinds of medical tests.

Many doctors and nurses had been coming in and out of my room to take care of me but it still seemed to be a mystery what was wrong with me. There still seemed to be more questions than answers.

As a result I was confused, scared and felt alone. I was just looking for answers.

As I stared out into the hall a woman appeared in my doorway in a white jacket. Although I had never seen her before, she radiated kindness.

She asked if she could come in and then asked me what was wrong. Apparently, I looked upset. I poured out my whole heart to her including my disbelief that I was here in the hospital and all my fears about what was happening to me.

In those few minutes, this woman brought peace and kindness and Grace into my hospital room and into my situation.

She talked with me about having faith that I was here in the hospital because I needed to be here in order for the doctors and nurses to figure out what was wrong with me and how to help me feel better so that I could go home. I don't know how she did it, but I felt more peaceful and calm than I had felt the entire time I was hospitalized. She brought this presence into the room that was so peaceful. And when she left I found that she had left that peace and presence behind with me.

When I was alone again, I was so grateful for her visit, and I still didn't even know who she was.

The next day she returned to my room and introduced herself to me as a professor at Becker College who was in charge of the student nurses. She asked if it would be okay if her students were to care for me as my student nurses. I was so grateful to have met her and to learn what she did in the hospital. I was sure that I wanted to be cared for by this caring woman's students.

After two weeks in the hospital it was decided by the doctors that I would be discharged from that hospital and sent to a Rehabilitation Hospital for further care.

In the meantime Dr. Enoh and I had become acquainted and had bonded over our mutual love for students and teaching and learning. Dr. Enoh promised to keep in touch with me and follow my progress as I continued in my health care journey. Each time I went back to the hospital for further testing I tried to get in touch with her.

Finally it was decided by my doctors that I would need open heart surgery in order to replace a damaged heart valve. Dr. Enoh helped encourage me through my panic and fear since I had never had any kind of surgery before.

Dr. Enoh came to visit me in the hospital after my open heart surgery. She continued to call me with encouragement and support and send me cards after I was released from the hospital to go home.

Later during my recovery I found out that Dr. Enoh was writing her autobiography and I thought "this is a book that needs to be written and read by many people as she is such a good example of a kind and generous and professional health care educator."

I cannot recommend this book more highly.

It is a privilege to know Dr. Enoh and to help her bring her story to the world. The world needs more people like her.

I hope the readers will learn from her story and carry it forward into their own lives. I hope her readers will be as blessed to know her from her book as I was when she first walked into my room.

Sincerely,
Kathleen M. Healy, Ph.D.

CHAPTER 1

The Beginning of My Life

I was born in the little village of Afaha Atai, Eket, in what was then Eastern Nigeria, in Africa. My parents, Samuel and Bella were peasant farmers who farmed their lands and raised livestock that included goats and chickens both for sale and for our food. Neither of my parents ever attended any school. As the youngest of their six children, I grew up outside with nature. The most modern thing I knew of then was the bicycle, which only rich people could afford in my village. For this reason, I never knew how to ride a bicycle since my parents could not afford one.

Our daily activities were helping our parents with farm work, doing house chores and going to school. The men were considered the sole breadwinners in my village. They were predominantly farmers. Very few men held jobs other than farming. If they did, they were petit traders, preachers, teachers, tailors, barbers, carpenters, hunters, and fishermen. Education then was mostly meant for boys; still, not many boys went to school. School was not popular for girls; they were raised to be homemakers only. Women in my village rarely held jobs outside the family. They were supposed to be provided for by their husbands. Their main responsibilities were to be married early, to care for their husbands, bear and raise children, help with farming and manage their homes. It was thought then, that none of what the women did required any form of schooling.

Our roads were footpaths since we did not have cars. In our village, there was no electricity, no telephones, no tap water, no flushable toilets, no radio or television. For toilets, we had pit latrines or a designated bush area nearby where each family disposed of personal waste. Bathrooms were a little thatched, fenced area behind the house with a small drain to rid the bath water onto the land beyond it. We fetched water from the river, which was about three miles away, for drinking and cooking.

Life then was simple, peaceful, and very close to nature. Moonlight was always greatly celebrated. Since there was no electricity, the moon was the only way the whole village could be lit at night. Children in my village played late into the night. Social events like native dances and men's society were carried out during the moonlight too. Today, many people do not even realize when the moon is out, whereas it was a big deal for us then in the early 1950's

Monday through Friday, some children were in school, the other children and their parents were at work or on the farm. Saturdays were big market and preparatory days for Sunday. Food was gathered from the farm and bought from the market since no store or market would be open on Sundays. People were up early to cook and clean their houses before going to church on Sunday morning. After church was recreational time for visiting family and friends, swimming, playing soccer (football) for the boys, and the braiding and fixing of hair for the women, getting ourselves ready for the work-week and school ahead. Most villagers did their laundry on Sunday afternoon by hand in the nearby river, since it was easier than trying to fetch enough water to do it at home.

There was a great sense of unity, trust and safety in our village. Everyone knew each other and took care of each other. We had mud houses with thatched roofs and bamboo doors, which were kept open during the day and only shut at night. It was never heard of, or even thought about that anybody would break into another's home. The only stealing that occurred occasionally was from the farms. Neighboring villagers would sometimes steal yams, cassava and some animals from other villages' farms.

Life then was based on an extended family system made up of great grandparents, grandparents, parents, children, grand and great grandchildren, nephews and nieces. As families grew bigger, they added more thatched closed houses to contain them. These clusters of houses identified each family. The women were "married out" of the extended family and the men "married into" the extended family. Men were considered the sole sustenance of the family lineage because they married into the family and maintained the family name. At this time, my culture placed much emphasis on having male children rather than female. A woman who only had girls was considered almost childless. This could be grounds for her husband to marry another woman so she could give him a male child. The husband could then decide to either keep or divorce the first wife. Because of their desire for a male heir, polygamy was very common during my childhood. The number of women a man married then also signified how wealthy he was. My uncle on my mother's side had four "official" wives. Each of them had their separate houses in his compound. He lived alone in the main building and had designated days for each of the wives to be there with him. When it was your day to spend time with your husband, you were responsible to cook and entertain him. The subsequently married wives had to be very respectful to the first wife. As a young child, I used to love visiting my uncle because he was very kind to me and had many children for me to play with. A family's strength then was based on the number of family members. I was born into this background so this is what I learned.

My mother had six children, five girls and one boy. The first child was a girl, followed by the only boy and four other girls. I did not know the ages or the age differences between my siblings because they were so much older than I was, since I was the last-born child. My father was a very peaceful man who loved my mother so much that it never bothered him that he had only one son and five daughters. I only heard my father bring this issue up once. The reaction from my father for having many daughters was, "I will never waste my energy, money and time to send a girl to school---it is a waste, it is just a waste. Once they get an education, they will leave the family to be married to a man who will benefit from all my hard work to put her through school. Is it worth it? No!" My mother, on the other hand, always stressed the importance of education for all, both boys and girls. Although school was expensive at all levels, primary and secondary, she worked extremely hard to put all of us through primary school.

There was no free education in Nigeria then. Primary school started from A, B, C (maybe the now preschool), then class one and two. After class two, you would progress to standard one through six. Therefore, it took nine years to complete primary school in Eastern Nigeria. The system was different in Northern Nigeria. There a student completed primary education in seven years. At the completion of primary education, you earned your "First School Leaving Certificate." Back then, secondary (high school) was not popular and we did not even have a high school nearby. It took five years to complete high school to earn your "West African Exam Council Certificate." My parents were able to send my brother and my three older sisters to primary school. My brother had been the only one who had continued on to high school. He went as far as the fourth year, although he had one more year to go, he stopped. I do not know why my brother did not complete high school in order to graduate. Four years of high school was viewed as a lot of education then, since it was enough to earn him a good paying job.

My brother's first job was teaching in a primary school, far away from my village, I was told. My two older sisters dropped out of primary school early to get married. My mother was not happy with their decisions, but they both did it anyway. My other two sisters completed primary school and later went into nursing school. Once my brother started working, he was able to help my mother pay for my immediate older sister Alice's primary education. This was a great relief for my mother, for my brother to help his sister. My sister in return went to live with him, served him and did all the chores in his home. It was part of our culture then to have "maids." The maids may or may not be a family member. Each maid could be paid either in cash or in kind. My sister Alice was going to be paid in kind. She would live at our brother's house and serve her brother while he in turn would take care of her including paying for her education. He would not give her any money for serving him; her only payment was her education.

Then my brother changed jobs from teaching. He got a new job as a postal clerk. He moved in rank in the postal services until he became the head-postmaster. After working there for a while, my mother pressured him to get married. He was her only son and she wanted grandchildren. Arranged marriages were still very common in my village. In an arranged marriage, it was the place of the man's family to approach the family of the young woman they would like their son to marry to ask her parents for permission for her hand in marriage to their son. If the young woman's family agreed, the man's family would bring gifts and a dowry to the young woman's family. Therefore, she would be betrothed or engaged to their son. The couple may not even have met each other before.

Their parents had made all of the arrangements. It was not the custom then, for the young woman's family to go to the man's family to ask their son's hand in marriage to their daughter.

The criteria for marriage was to have a good family background and wealth, which was mostly possession of farmlands and livestock. Once all the arrangements were completed between the two families, a date for the traditional marriage was set. The young woman's family would then give the husband- to-be a list of what they wanted to be brought on the traditional marriage date. The husband-to-be and his family must bring all that was on the list including the "bride price" or "dowry" and assorted drinks. The traditional marriage day was full of fun and merry making carried out by the bride's family. At the end of the day, the bride would go home with her new husband and his family for the first time.

Arranged marriage then almost looked like selling the young woman—her parents felt like they raised her to be married out, so their compensation for raising her was what they received during the marriage ceremony. My brother had an arranged marriage. My mother chose her son's wife, then paid her family the dowry and gave whatever her family had on their list. She completed the traditional marriage protocol before sending for her son to come and take his wife-to-be, in 1956. I believe this was the first time they had met. My brother came home to our village and met his wife-to-be, then married her and brought her back with him to the big city where he was working. He accepted my mother's choice for him without any question.

By this time, my two older sisters were both married and living with their children in my village. Their families were within walking distance from our house, so their children were frequently at our house. I always visited them too, and sometimes I would spend a couple of weeks with either of my sisters. They were very good to me and I always felt very comfortable with my sisters, and even felt spoiled a bit. Sometimes, to avoid errands at home, I would take off to one of my sisters' houses. Being the baby of my family, I liked my sisters' houses more because they had young children I could play with. I had grown up almost like an only child because I came so late to my older parents. My siblings were all grown and gone out of the house, and this made me lonely at home.

I had such a wonderful mother who never raised her voice to me or punished me. She was soft- spoken, a woman of few words. My father slapped me once on my back because he sent me to go and buy tobacco for him, and I took what he thought, was an excessively long time to get back. My mother was very upset with him for that. I will always remember that incident because that was the first and the last time I was ever punished by either of my parents. They had a lot of patience with me; I was just a child and did not know any better. My mom would explain things to me instead of yelling at or spanking me. This made me very close to her and I appreciated her a lot then and even more as I got older.

On one occasion when some of my older siblings came over, we were having supper together and one of them teased me saying, the reason I was so tiny was because I came so late in my parents' life, so they who were born earlier, took all the better part of mom and dad. My sister said that was why they were all bigger and taller than I was. Mom gave me a hug and said, "Leave her alone! It is not a matter of size or beauty. It is what you do with yourself." She continued to explain to them and to me that she was aware that she had me late in her life and that's why she named me Enoh-Abasi, which means God's gift. She said, "If it were humanly controlled, I would not have had you; they would have thought I was too old to have a child." Yes, I was small as a child and I am still a petit woman today, but mom's saying came true. (Speak good words to your children; it does have a positive impact on them). My home was very peaceful, I never heard my parents argue or have any forms of fighting among themselves. We were very poor, but happy. We did not have much, but we always had each other.

CHAPTER 2

Leaving Home for the First Time

My earliest memory of my older brother was when he visited our home for a couple of weeks on vacation from the post office. By this time, he was married and had a baby girl. I was about seven years old. During that visit, I expressed to my mother my interest to follow my brother back to wherever he lived. I wanted to go and babysit for him. My mother's reply to that was, "If that's what you want, go ahead." I did not say anything to my brother about my intent to follow him back to the city, and my mother did not talk to him about it either. One evening, my brother told my mother and me to sit down and said, "Well, I am very willing to sponsor Enoh in school if she will go back with me so she can help with the baby and do some chores at home." I was so thrilled that I could not contain my happiness. My mother responded, "Yes, she will go with you. She has already expressed her interest, I just had not told you about it. I am going to miss Enoh a lot, but I am not going to hold her back from her wishes." My brother returned to work in Gusau, a city in the Northern part of Nigeria, taking his family and me with him.

At seven years of age, I could not imagine then where life was taking me. I was very happy to leave home to go to the "Big City." The final day came; I took the few clothes I had in a raffia bag. I had never had a pair of shoes, so I walked barefoot, and left home with my brother, his wife and the baby. We travelled by foot, passing several villages before we got to a transportation station (motor park). There were several taxis, cars, mini buses, trailer trucks, motorcycles etc. There were many people coming in and leaving to different destinations. To me, the transportation station seemed extremely busy! I was watching all that was going on keenly since this was my first time ever leaving my village. My brother went to negotiate with a lorry (truck) driver for the fare for his family and me. I had no idea what he paid for our trip, but he came back with tickets for all of us. We waited for about an hour for the lorry to be loaded with other passengers before we boarded and took off. This was the first time I had ever seen a lorry, so it was quite exciting to be riding in it!

The lorry took us to Aba, another big city where we were going to board a train. My brother then bought train tickets for all of us. I was still observing everything around me. On our way, I had seen cars, motorcycles, bicycles, and many people going about their business. These were all new to me since we did not have these vehicles in my village. It was late that evening before the train came. There were electric lights everywhere and I could not figure it out since the lights were not coming from the moon and they were a lot brighter than the moonlight. I was full of questions over new things I had never seen before. "How are the nights lit here in the city without the moonlight? What are the lights called and how do they come on?" I asked my brother. My brother told me that the way the light was turned on, was called electricity. He tried to explain how it worked to me but I did not understand. He tried to answer most of my questions as best he could. I was amazed at how the city could be so different and complicated compared to the simple village life I knew.

Finally, our train arrived at the station. It was a very long structure on wheels, linked coach by coach to each other. It blew a loud whistle that startled me before it came to a screeching stop. Some people came out while others went in. We were one of the groups that were boarding the train at this station. As I went in, I noticed that each of the coaches had compartments with seats like benches on each side and a passage in the middle where people could get to their seats. My brother helped me in and found a seat on the bench for me. I sat down and my imagination soared. "This is wonderful," I thought. Each of the train's compartments had about ten benches and five people in each seat. I sat by the window so I could see wherever or whatever the train passed by. There were toilets in the train but no water to flush them. I did not understand how the waste products were disposed of, but the train was quite clean in my opinion. It was to be a three-day journey before we would arrive at our final destination.

On our arrival, everybody got out of the train since this was the end of the line. We retrieved our luggage and I helped carry our suitcases as we walked the two miles to my brother's house. This was a very big city with many people going about their business on foot, bicycles, motorcycles or cars. This city had electricity too. At this point, I thought to myself, "Could my little village ever grow into a big city like this? No, I do not think so, I pondered." When I arrived at my brother's, it was a very nice mud house with one bedroom and a living room. The inside was painted white, so it really looked nice compared to the houses we were living in at my village. It had windows and real doors. The kitchen was built separately, so the house was not stuffy with smoke compared to our village houses where wood fires were used for cooking within the houses and there were no windows for ventilation. Also adding to the smoke, were kerosene lamps used instead of electricity. I thought, "This house is really cool," I liked it a lot.

By the second week of staying with my brother and his family, I became homesick. The beautiful house, the good and abundant food and the better living environment meant very little at this point to me. I missed my home, parents, sisters, nephews, and nieces so much. Everything my brother and his wife did to cheer me up only made me sadder and more depressed. I wanted to go back home! I cried so much silently, I could not eat. My brother and his wife tried unsuccessfully to find out what was bothering me. I felt I could not tell them. In my mind, telling them that I missed home was not going to solve my problem, so I kept to myself saying very little or nothing. I said to myself, "this was my choice to come here, so I have to deal with it." If someone had forced me to go with my brother, I would have been blaming that person now. I did not even know my brother before, to my recollection. This home visit was the first time I had met him so he was like a stranger to me. The gap between his age and mine made him seem more like a father than a brother. He was approximately twenty-five years older than I was. This age difference and the fact that I was with my brother as a stranger for the first time made me even more homesick.

I was still in this homesickness mode when my brother enrolled me in a nearby Catholic school. Once I began going to school I started feeling better. I started making friends and I enjoyed my classes. At the beginning of the school, I had a language problem. Before, I had only spoken and understood our native language, which we used at home. I had no knowledge of the English language at all. All the schools in this city were taught in English. Since most of the children spoke different languages, English was used as a universal language. As a child, it did not take me too long, neither did I find it too hard to pick up English and the other unofficial languages spoken by the other children plus the local language spoken by the people in this city. For this reason, I became multilingual. I spoke English, Ibo, Hausa and Calabar fluently and a little bit of Yoruba. These were the main languages spoken in Nigeria within each state and there were dialects within these languages. English remained the official language used in Nigeria, spoken in schools, offices and any other official places. I adjusted well and loved school a lot because of my new friends and learning new things. Life at home was all right. I helped with the little I could do and became more cheerful. I was struggling in school until the second year when I had the English language down pat. I started doing very well in school and this made me happy. I rather comforted myself at this point, thinking, "Maybe it was worth leaving home at 7 years old to have this new life."

CHAPTER 3

The Accident

I n my young mind, I had to "move on" even though I missed
my mom so much. My brother and his wife were very caring
to me and I appreciated them. I enjoyed taking care of the
baby girl who was about nine months old at this time. She was
crawling and could pull herself up by holding on to objects.

One evening, my brother's wife called me to bring the
baby to be bathed. She had already poured water in a basin to
bathe the baby, so when I came, I just put the baby in the basin
feet first, and the baby let out a scream. I picked her right
out and put my hand in to test the water only to realize that
her mother did not cool the water to an appropriate tempera-
ture before she summoned me to bring the baby for her bath.
Realizing what happened, I started crying and shouting for
help right away. My brother's wife came out of the house running and grabbed the baby from me. Noticing what happened;
she took the baby inside the house and treated her with a rem-
edy I did not know. I was still crying, feeling horrible at what

had happened even though it was an accident. Thankfully, the baby sustained only a superficial scald on her right foot that healed without taking the baby to the hospital and she did not have any lasting damage. It did not take long either for her scar to disappear. I felt so relieved and thankful to God that the baby was all right.

From the time of that accident, my brother's wife's attitude changed towards me. She started yelling at me unnecessarily, hitting me for any reason or no reason at all. She became extremely physically and verbally abusive to me. This was confusing to me, "Was she still upset with me because of the accident with the baby? Did she think I hurt the baby on purpose?" Many thoughts ran through my mind. I became so scared and had nowhere to go and no one to turn to. I could not talk to any of my friends or my teachers at school about my home situation.

As if the physical and verbal abuse was not bad enough, my brother's wife started to refuse to give me food. The worst was when she would not allow me to eat breakfast before leaving for school. I had to walk several miles to get to school, which started at 8:00 AM. By noontime, I was so hungry and weak that I could not hold my head up in class. During our lunch break, I would walk weakly into the school garden or any nearby farms to find and pick some nuts to eat. The nuts and some water would sustain me until school was dismissed at 2:00 PM. My brother's wife expected me to run home several miles within seven to ten minutes after school. I was too hungry and weak to walk fast or run home. If I got home later than her expected time, she would hit me and deny me food until suppertime. She had given birth to more children by now. At suppertime, she would give me only what was left over from her other children after they had eaten for the day. I ate out of necessity to survive but sometimes the food would be so old and bad that irrespective of how hungry I was, I couldn't eat it, I would throw it out. Whenever my brother's wife found out that I threw the bad food out, she would hit me so much for wasting her food. She would ask me, "Do you know how hard it is to earn the money used to buy the food you just wasted?" This woman had never worked since she got married to my brother. She had no job, she totally depended on her husband, so, as a child, and I could not understand what she meant by "how hard it is to earn money." I learned to survive from what I picked from the school garden because I was never sure that I would eat when I got home from school.

One of the worst days of my torment was when I woke up one morning not feeling well. I had a fever. I did not tell anybody about it because I felt it wouldn't matter if I did tell them, so I kept it to myself and left for school. I thought, "I would rather go to school sick than stay home." I left for school that morning as usual without being allowed to have breakfast. When I came back from school, still without eating, I had to start my chores. My first chore that day was to wash a bucketful of soaked, dirty, flannel baby diapers by hand. Immediately I took off my school uniform, and I got started. As I was washing the diapers outside behind the house, my brother's wife was giving her new three-month-old baby a bath inside the house. Her oldest daughter stood at the doorway watching me wash the diapers and she wanted to get me in trouble, so she said to her mother, "Mom, Enoh is playing." The girl was laughing as she was saying this. She knew that she was lying and that her mother would believe her. She knew I was going to be punished. I knew too that even if I were to defend myself, I was still going to be punished. I said a prayer for the Lord to give me the strength to take the beating that I was going to receive and if it was unbearable, I prayed, "God please just take my life so that I can rest in peace." After this prayer, I made a conscious decision not to say a word to defend myself when my brother's wife called me in.

She called and I went in. She had the baby on her lap as she was just completing his bath. She asked me, "Were you playing instead of washing the diapers?" Not a word from me, I stood with both arms folded across my chest. She got so mad because I did not answer her question and she wrapped the baby up in a blanket, put him in the bed, came over in a rage, and started beating me. I did not move or even flinch. Not feeling well and not eating all day did not make the situation any easier. I thought to myself that this would be my last day alive. I stood still, receiving her beating without crying or uttering any word and this really infuriated her the more. She dragged me outside the house and pushed me onto the concrete blocks that were there. I sustained a large cut on my left shin, it was bleeding profusely, and she said to me, "Good for you, that serves you right." It was at this point that I spoke for the first time. I said to her, "You know what? You can do whatever you want with my flesh, but you cannot touch or break my spirit, so keep hitting me if it gives you so much pleasure and satisfaction." At this point, I was ready to give up and die, but instead she left me alone.

When my brother came home from work, his wife told him what happened that evening with me. He called me in to question me. I thought, "It isn't going to make any difference what I say," he is going to take the side of his wife, so I decided not to answer any of his questions. He said to me, "I am taking a decision on you since you insulted my wife. Get out of my face." I walked out without giving a damn to what my brother had said. In my childish mind, I knew and believed that my brother and his wife were not God-like, and that what I was going through in their house was temporary. I said to myself, "It will surely end one day, if I survive." This cannot last forever even though it seemed then, like the end would never come.

I received scars and bruises all over my body because of the physical abuse from my brother's wife. My face had scratches from her fingernails digging into me. My ears were so scarred and sore, that, at one point I was afraid that this woman could actually pull my ears off my head. If I laughed, my brother's wife would smack me across my face and say, "Shut your stinky mouth." It got to a point where I just stopped laughing in my brother's house. It was not worth the punishment I was going to receive for laughing. On one occasion, I was walking out of the house. My brother's wife pulled me so suddenly and unexpectedly that I hit the right side of my forehead on the doorframe, sustaining a large cut. It bled profusely and it hurt a lot. I was crying and she said to me, "Good for you, I wish your head was split into two." I still have the scar from this incident on my forehead. The physical and the emotional abuse continued, and grew worse as I got older.

One good thing was, whenever my brother's wife hit me so badly, I never continued doing any chores for the rest of that day. I would just find an isolated corner to stay and cry, pray, sing, talk to God, and think a lot about my mother back home in my village. This also meant no food for me the rest of that day. This was when I developed an interest in singing and I still sing a lot most of the time to this day. My songs then were predominantly songs of comfort and praise. Today, I sing songs of praise and victory for what the Lord has done for me. I had to go through this harsh punishment a couple of times a week, yet, miraculously; the Lord always strengthened me. I would go to bed without food at night, yet, I would wake up okay the following morning. I used to talk to God a lot even though I did not really understand how He worked. I believed He heard me because I always felt His presence with me.

One day the thought of running away to go back home to my mother occurred to me - I started making plans. Then I realized how far we were from home - three days on the train and one in the lorry, a total of four days. I had no money and I was too young to travel home by myself. This made me discouraged and depressed. It was at this point that I totally surrendered to Jesus, without fully understanding what that meant. I would talk to Him, prayed, praised and sang. The result of this new change brought me tremendous inner peace, calmness, an uplifted spirit, and greater physical strength. I realized then that even when I was starved, I was neither hungry, weak, angry nor depressed. I did all my chores cheerfully because Jesus comforted me and took all my burdens from me, giving me the grace to go on. In retrospect, Kelly Clarkson's song says, "What doesn't kill you makes you stronger, stronger." I implicitly believe in the wording of this song. Even though this song was not written then, it was still applicable. I came out of this situation so strong, that I probably wouldn't be who or where I am today if I did not go through all that abuse in my brother's house.

In my third year of living with my brother, he decided to take his whole family back to our home, in the village on vacation. At first, I was afraid that he was going to leave me behind in the city but he did not, and we all went home. It was heavenly to see my dear parents and the rest of my family. I tasted freedom once more. I was so happy and determined never to go back with my brother. We spent a couple of weeks at my parents' home and the last week, I whispered to my mom that I could never go back again with my brother. I had already told mom all I could about what I went through and showed her the scars and bruises all over my body. I had expected her to be very upset and tell my brother's wife off, but she did not do as I expected. Mom was quiet about what she heard and the evidence of abuse all over my body. I could see the pain and the anger on her face.

Three days to the end of my brother's vacation, my mother called me and said, "Sit down my beloved daughter; I need to have a talk with you." My heart started racing, I became a little anxious, but the trust I had in my mother gave me the hope that whatever she had to say would be for my good, now and in the future because she loved me. I sat down, eager to hear what she had to say. Mom started by saying, "My dear daughter, I have heard all you have said, I have seen all the scars and bruises on your body as evidence, yet, you will go back with your brother. He is your brother. If he and his wife kill you by any means, they will be answerable to God in heaven. You do not quit when things get tough, you have to complete the work that you have started, to gain a true lasting reward. Quitters never win and winners never quit. Go back with your brother and help him with his children. If you endure to the end, then you will receive a crown of victory says the Bible." I slumped over in my chair. Tears filled my eyes, rolling down my face, and I could not utter a word to my mother. She pulled me over to herself, gave me a hug and tried wiping the tears from my eyes and face. Nothing would console me. After three years of torment, I had finally tasted freedom, which would soon be gone! I was very depressed; the endless tears kept rolling down my cheeks until the day of our departure came. On that day, Mom and my two sisters escorted us by walking to the transportation station with us. Once I said goodbye to my family, I climbed into the lorry, then, I lost it totally. I cried so much that I became sick on our way back from that vacation. I didn't hold it against my mother for telling me to go back with my brother. At the same time, I did not understand why she had made such a decision.

CHAPTER 4

The Miracle

Once we had returned to my brother's house from that vacation, my brother's wife taunted me and did whatever she pleased with me. My brother never bothered to inquire why his wife hated and mistreated me so much; neither did he give me any form of comfort or reassurance. It came to a point that my brother's wife started interfering with my going to school once she realized that I liked school and was doing well. She would bring out cooking pots and pans for me to scrub at the time I should have left for school. By the time I finished, it was always too late to go to school and she would say, "You have to go to school whether you like it or not." She would throw my school bag outside on the ground and say, "If you don't go to school, that's your fault and you will stay outside until school is over. You can't step into this house until after school." I would then be over an hour late for school. Sometimes I would be defiant and stay outside from 8:00 AM until 2:00 PM doing nothing. My only joy when she started messing around with my education was that the harder she tried to ruin it for me, the better I did in school and she did not like that at all.

Then, my brother was transferred from Gusau to Kaura Namoda, another nearby town in Northern Nigeria. Although he was not sympathetic to my situation at home, my brother always wanted the best education for me. Therefore, he did not want me to switch schools, since the following year was going to be my last year in primary school. Instead, he arranged for me to move in with a friend of his and their family. I knew this family but did not know what to expect moving in to their house to spend more than a year with them. My brother moved me in with them first, in order to be sure I was settled before he left with his own family to Kaura Namoda. This new family welcomed me warmly. They had two young daughters ages four and six. Living for a year with this family was wonderful. They were very nice to me. I helped with chores and caring for the two children. I paid very short visits to my brother's house during my school vacation. The break I got from my brother by staying with this family was very rewarding. I learned from them that kindness and good treatment increases productivity. It increases people's eagerness to do more. I was very happy, and was doing well both in school and at home. It was a very peaceful family where I felt appreciated. Their little children loved me, and I loved them too.

I finished primary school and then took the national certificate exam, which I passed. Next, I started the process of applying to high schools for admission. My brother was very helpful in this process. He was supportive with funding for my education and I appreciated it a lot. My brother said, "I would have borrowed money to send you to high school even if I couldn't afford it because you are such a bright child." That may have been the only positive compliment I ever received throughout my stay at my brother's house.

My brother wanted me to take entrance exams to a couple of high schools just to be sure I would be accepted into one. When his wife heard this, she said to him, "If you spend all your money for the entrance exam and Enoh is accepted into a high school, what are you going to use to pay for her tuition? Let her take an exam for only one school. If she fails, then that will be it for her education." I knew that she was not happy for me to go to high school. My brother listened to his wife's advice and had me take an entrance exam to only one school and that was it.

I thought there was no point in worrying over what I had no control over, so I did the only thing I knew how to do, I prayed. My prayer that day was; "Dear Lord, you've always been there for me. You've never disappointed me. Make it possible that whatever number of candidates that would be accepted for this school let me be one of them, to your honor and glory Amen." This was a federal entrance exam. If you passed, then you would go to the school of your choice in whatever state it was located in Nigeria, for a final written exam and then an interview. Eight weeks after the federal entrance exam, the results were out and I passed! No words could express the feelings within me; I was so thrilled! I thought I was going to burst open with joy! I could finally see my freedom coming - going to a boarding high school. This meant I would live at the high school and not with my brother and his family-WOW! However, it was not over yet. I still had to pass the written exam and then the interview at the school of my choice. I was at peace knowing that I had placed my future in God's hands.

Two weeks after the result of the federal entrance exam, I received a letter from the school of my choice informing me of the date, time and place for both my final exam and interview. My brother was very happy for me. He made all the transportation arrangements for me to travel to my home village by myself since the school was in my home state - Cross River State (the former Eastern Nigeria). I finally could envision a light at the end of the tunnel!

I travelled by myself for three days on the same train that had brought us to this city, and then took the lorry, arriving home to my parents on the fourth day. I spent three days at home with Mom and Dad in the village before heading to the high school on the scheduled date for the exam and interview.

My mom asked my immediate older sister, Alice, who was then 10 years older, to travel with me to the school. I was surprised that she would ask my sister to come with me for only a three-hour journey, since I had just made a four days journey on my own. Before we left home, I gave Alice all the money I had. On our way, she remarked that I was going to an interview without a pair of shoes. "Yes," I said, "I have never had a pair of shoes." My brother and his family had many pairs of shoes, not me. She seemed disturbed about this. Then I said to her, "Do not worry about that, I do not think that any reasonable mature adult would fail a kid who has brains but not shoes. If the interviewer or anyone asks me about it, I will reply to them saying, `I am on my way to possess many pairs of shoes and many other things than shoes in life, if I am accepted into this high school." My sister responded, "Well, I do not like the idea of you going to an interview without any shoes on, that could make them fail you." I answered her, "I don't think so, besides, I don't have a choice. The money I gave you is only for our transportation. It would not be wise to buy shoes which is not a necessity, and be stranded, which would be very risky."

Then I remember my sister taking me to a store in one of the cities on our way to the high school and she bought me my very first pair of shoes when I was thirteen years old. They were very nice brown open-toe sandals. I was very happy about it although it would not have bothered me if I had no shoes on for the interview. I was sure that getting an education would meet all my needs and then I may even be able to help others. Above all, it was going to get me out of my brother's house a lot sooner than by any other means.

My sister Alice and I finally arrived at the boarding high school. We had been informed that the exams and the interview were going to take three days. The candidates' names were arranged in alphabetical order by their last names. My last name started with a U, so I was in the last group. I finished on the third day at about 4:00 PM. At this point, I was not worried if I was going to be accepted or not. Instead, I was relieved that both the exam and the interview were finally over.

The boarding high school provided us with meals throughout our stay. That evening after supper, I decided to relax, look around the school, and learn as much information as I could about the school from the older students who were brought in to help during the interviewing process. The senior girls told us about the school routine, the kind of food that the school provided for them, the courses offered, types of sports they played and social events. I got excited when I learned of all the possibilities this school had for me.

We had come during vacation time for the high school. Alice and I went to bed around 8:00 PM that evening. All our things were packed in preparation for our departure the following morning. At 3:30 AM that morning, my sister woke me up saying, "Enoh, there is something very important I could not tell you earlier, but I have to tell you right now. Wake up! This is serious." I could not imagine what was wrong - I thought she was joking. "What is it?" I asked. "We have five pennies left. We have no money to pay our way back home." I sat up in bed, my sleepy eyes and head woke up sharply. "What!" We needed about thirty naira for both of us to get home. My sister continued, "I did not want to tell you earlier because I knew you had exams to take. I have been worried sick, most especially because you warned me about buying the shoes with the transport money."

Now I was fully awake, trying to grasp what my sister had just told me and to figure out what to do next. First, I got up and knelt at my bedside to pray. In my prayer, I commended the day ahead into the Lord's hand, knowing that He alone would be able to get us home safely. I did not worry about how God was going to do it, I simply prayed and believed that God would help us. Since this was our situation now, we would have to leave early. We needed to walk about twelve miles to the city where we would find a lorry that was home bound. I got up, took a bath and began to dress up. My sister was still sitting where she was at the beginning of our conversation, looking very helpless. "Get up and be ready, we have to be out of here by 5:00 AM," I said. "Walking, we may arrive in the city between 9:00 and 11:00 AM I hope. You have to be strong! It is not going to be an easy day and we do not have any choice!" My sister got up, bathed and dressed up and we left at 5:00 AM.

It was still dark outside. We had no idea how safe or risky it was for us to walk in this part of the country, but we had no choice, so we did. About 6:30 AM, taxis carrying the rest of the candidates from the exam and interview from the high school started passing us as we walked, heading back to the city. About six miles to the city, one of the taxis stopped beside us. A girl stuck her face out of the window. It was one of the senior students who had stayed to help the candidates during the interview. She was in charge of our dormitory so she recognized me and asked the taxi driver to stop for her to check on us to make sure we were okay. I quickly assessed the taxi to see if there were empty seats. Too bad, the taxi was packed full, so there was no point in asking them for help. I assured her that we were okay to be walking. She believed me and they drove on. About 9:00 AM, we finally arrived in the city. I was thanking God that we had arrived safely.

We were then supposed to get another transport from this city to take us to our parents' home. This would take about three hours by lorry and about two hours by taxi. We were to be dropped off at a main street and then would need to walk another hour on a dirt road to get home. My sister was so distraught, anxious and worried since she had no idea how we were going to get home without money. I was her little sister and my mom was going to hold her accountable if anything bad happened to us. I looked calm and collected but in my heart, I was praying for a miracle. In my prayers I said, "Lord, you've done it for me numerous times. I believe and trust you will do it again. I am helpless and completely leaning on you to take us home safely." I stood still, gazing upwards as I delivered my silent prayer request to God. I completed my prayers, turned to check on my sister and she was walking towards an unknown man, a total stranger. "What is she doing?" I pondered.

When she approached the stranger, she started talking to him about our problem. I ran and pushed her away from him, making sure she was not going back to him or to any other person for help. I made sure I kept her right by me. I said to her, "Why can't you trust God to solve our problem in a miraculous way? Don't you know that He can meet all our needs? Do not ever lose faith, trust Him, and see what He will do for us. God has never disappointed me, so I trust Him all the way." I now sounded like a preacher. My sister started crying. She felt so bad because she was the cause of our predicament. I told her to never mind the cause; that this was meant to happen so that the Lord would prove to us that He cares unconditionally for his children. At this point, my sister was sobbing uncontrollably saying, "If anything happens to us Mom is going to blame me. I should have known better."

As we stood together at the roadside, I was observing the activities all around us. From this observation, I noticed that around 11:15 AM, many cars and trucks started passing us in our homeward direction, so I decided to cross over to stand on the opposite side of the road, since this seemed to be the side for homebound cars or lorries and trucks. Once I had said my prayers, I was very peaceful and reassured that the Lord would provide us with transportation. I kept watching out for any lorry heading home. The exposure of travelling with my brother had made me aware of recognizable names of lorries that were homebound. Many cars and lorries passed by, I was watching closely to see if I could recognize any of them. About 12:00 noon, I noticed a lorry with a name I recognized coming. I shouted to my sister to hurry over while I stepped right out to where the driver could see me, waving my hands for him to stop. He saw us and stopped the lorry saying, "Jump in quick." We did, without any hesitation. There were other passengers in the lorry but there was enough room for us. The driver asked us why we came to this city. I answered him saying, "I came for an interview for secondary school admission." He was very happy for me since education was rare and considered very valuable in my village. Once we settled in the lorry, I started praising God silently, thanking Him for another miracle. My sister was still teary but relieved that we were on our way home at last. Finally, we were on our way home to our family in the village!

The lorry driver dropped all the other passengers off at the transportation station and then, surprisingly, he drove us right to our house. Mom was home and she would not let the lorry driver go until he had supper with us. She prepared a quick supper and we all ate together. The lorry driver never asked us for any money. We thanked him for being so kind to help and to have gone out of his way to drop us off at our house. It would have taken us another hour to walk from the motor park to our house. After all was said and done, I ran to my room, and then went on my knees to deliver my official thankful prayers to the Lord for the miracle He performed for us. Neither Alice nor I told mom what happened. This was a secret my sister and I kept between us. I pulled my sister aside and said to her, "See, you have to learn to trust God in all your ways. He will never disappoint you. Today, He has proven to you how He cares even when we screw up." We sat with our parents around the fire that evening and talked about almost everything except what actually happened that day.

Now that I was back from my exam and interview for the boarding high school, I had one more week to spend at home with my parents before going back to my brother's house in the North. My other sister Amelia heard of a late entrance exam to another nearby high school and asked me to take the exam. Late entrance exams were only conducted when schools did not have an adequate number of qualified candidates coming in for the following semester. I was reluctant to take it because I had faith in God that He would get me into the only high school I already applied to. My sister said to me, "You do not have anything to lose by having a second choice." "Okay," I said. I got ready and I went to this high school (Salvation Army Secondary School, Akai) on the scheduled date and time for the late entrance exam. This high school, which was considered "nearby," was about thirteen miles away from my village, so I walked both ways there. When I got to the high school, I told the teacher who was going to conduct the exams that I needed to be interviewed on that same day since I would be travelling back to the North of my country in a couple of days. I would not be available on the scheduled interview date. He agreed and so, set the time for the interview to be immediately after the written exam. I appreciated this, and the interview went well. I left this nearby school assured that I was accepted, and went back to my parents' home. I enjoyed the final one week I spent at home with my parents. I was thinking that going back to the North where my brother was living was not scary any more to me since I was now living with the other family.

CHAPTER 5

My Freedom at Last

I got ready and left my parents' home, going back to the North to our family friends and their two daughters. It was going to be just a short time before leaving them for the boarding high school. I was thrilled. When I came back from the high school exam and interview, I then also had to prepare for my final elementary school exams. I took those exams and I passed.

It was hard to say goodbye to our family friends that I had spent my last school year with. I fell in love with their two little girls and I was going to miss them a lot. That family was very good to me and I enjoyed my stay with them. They were very happy for me to be gaining an admission into a reputable high school. It was a Saturday morning when we had to say our goodbyes and part ways. I thought, "This might be the last time I will ever see them."

I came back from the family friends' home to my brother's house just to spend a couple of weeks. The result of my second choice nearby high school exam was mailed out to me and I passed. I was not very happy with this because my mind was all set and all my hopes and aspirations were still for my first choice boarding high school, Union Secondary School, Ibiaku. Finally, the letter came from my first choice high school and I passed that exam! I was so happy, so thrilled beyond anyone's imagination. My true freedom was here at last—free, free, free at last!

I had skipped two grades in my primary school, so my brother thought I was too young now to go to high school. This I strongly protested. "I can handle it! Why should I be held back?" He gave in to me and said, "If you feel you can handle it, then there is no point for me to hold you back." I was so relieved. The two schools had both sent their prospectus (school information and requirements) and the date the schools were going to start with my test results. Thankfully, my brother also preferred my first choice boarding high school even though it was farther away from my home compared to my second choice high school and it was more expensive. My first choice high school was an all-girls, boarding, private school and my second choice high school was a co-ed school for both boys and girls. Some of the students were boarders and others could live outside the school to reduce their cost. I was so happy that my brother did not change his mind about sending me to my first choice high school. He then had to notify my second choice high school – Salvation Army Secondary School, Akai, that I was not coming, so that another candidate could be accepted in my place.

We had been sent a list of requirements for my first choice high school and my brother started buying the things that were on the list: a suitcase, six simple cotton dresses, a pair of dressing shoes, school sandals, sneakers for sports and pocket money. Wow, I thought, "I am going to be loaded with clothes, shoes and money!" It was overwhelming to me when I saw the list. The school had indicated that I must have all the items listed, and that they were going to check to make sure I had the required items on arrival.

My brother was planning to send me to my village early so that I could spend that Christmas at home with my parents before leaving for boarding high school in January. I thought "the Lord did not only open doors for me; He was making it heavenly on earth for me so I could first go to see my parents and family before I left for the high school! Wow, could life be any better than this?" I was in my own glory, it felt so, so good that I vowed never to let go of my newfound joy and freedom brought through education. I felt great for the few weeks I had, back at my brother's house before leaving to boarding high school. It did not matter what was going on around me, I was in my own world, keeping a very low profile.

The following Saturday was going to be my last day at my brother's house. We were supposed to leave home at 6 AM for the train station since my brother was going to walk me there. All the preparations were completed; I could hardly sleep on Friday night. It seemed like the longest night of my life! I had said goodbye to my nephews and nieces Friday evening, knowing that they may not be awake to see me so early on

Saturday morning. This was good, as it made it less emotional for me. By this time, my brother had four children under the age of ten. The youngest child then was about three years old.

On December 15, 1963, at 5:45 AM, I stepped outside, turned back and took a good look at my brother's house, where I was tortured and starved for years. I took a couple of deep breaths and then a sigh of relief, feeling that I had gained my freedom at last. It was hard to believe that this day had finally come. I thought to myself "Oh well, if it is a dream, it is a good one and if it is real, I will certainly grab it and run with it!"

As I stood there, lost in my imagination, with the suitcase in my hand, my brother came out of the house to walk me to the train station to see me off. It took about 45 minutes for us to walk silently to the train station. I carried my suitcase on my head. My brother bought my train ticket and we waited for half an hour, without a word to each other, before the train arrived. I thanked my brother and said goodbye to him before boarding the train. It seemed more real now that I was out of my brother's house for good. I was ecstatic, so happy, I could not contain myself, laughing and crying hysterically at the same time as the train started moving away from the station. I thought, "Education is hard but its reward is worth working hard for." I love school; education brings you a step further for good and progress in life. My love for the one thing that brought my freedom a lot sooner than I anticipated, education, remains the love of my life.

It was a four- day journey before I arrived at my village. My parents, sisters, nephews and nieces were all waiting to welcome me back. They were so happy to see me and I was very happy to see them too. I spent about two weeks at home with my parents before heading off to my new boarding high school. During this time, I enjoyed my family and the friends I had at home. I told my mother as much as I could about what I went through at my brother's house. Some of the stories brought tears to both our eyes. When I was done talking, my mother said to me, "It is better that you endured to the end, God will surely reward you, and the rest of your life is going to be better than the beginning. As hard as it was for me to let you go back with your brother when you came home on that vacation, I thought and prayed about it before asking you to go back again with him. I knew he could afford to send you to school and I was not able to give you that. Another advantage you had by going with your brother was getting out of our little village to the big city where you were exposed to better opportunities. Now you are leaving for a secondary school in a few days. I could not afford that for you, and looking around, most of your age mates have not measured up to you. It was not easy then for both of us. The ending is great. I hope you are excited about going to a boarding high school. When you are done, you are going to get a very good job." She gave me a big hug and said, "I hope you will forgive me, I was only looking out for a better future for you, which as a child, you did not realize then. These were the reasons why I made you go back with your brother after that vacation." I said, "I forgive you, Mom," giving her a hug.

That Christmas was a great time for our family. Our house was decorated; we woke up early on Christmas day to cook special food- pounded yam and goat meat soup, rice and stew and pepper soup. Then we went to church. After the church service, my family gathered at our house for the celebration. There were entertainers all over the village, people had fun and it was joyful. I had not been at my village for Christmas for many years. This was refreshing and I was very happy.

CHAPTER 6

Going to Boarding High School

I n January 1964, it was time to head to my new boarding high school. This was the first time I was going to be on my own, living at school, away from all my family and friends. I did not know what to expect. I was very excited to be leaving for high school, ready to adjust to the new experience and environment. I decided then that I would do whatever it would take me to be successful at school. I gathered all the items the school had on their list, which my brother had bought for me, and a few personal items and began my journey to high school. My Mom and my sister, Amelia, saw me off at the transportation station. We hugged and said our goodbyes as I climbed into the lorry. They waited until the lorry took off as they waved to me. Three hours later, I arrived at my boarding high school.

My new school, Union Secondary School, Ibiaku, Ikot Ekpene in the then Cross River State, Nigeria, was an all girl's private missionary institution. On arrival at the campus, I was welcomed by one of the senior students assigned to direct me on what to do and where to go. Each of the new students had an assigned senior student to help them on that first day. This was very helpful, none of us felt lost, since we would be oriented to the school campus.

The first thing our senior students did was to take us to our assigned dormitories and then we picked our beds on a first-come-first-served basis. There were fourteen beds in each dormitory, seven on both sides, with a passage in the middle. In between each bed was a nightstand, one for each student. There were no curtains or any provision for privacy between the students' beds. It was just an open dormitory with beds on both sides. At the end of the dorm room was a closet for our suitcases, called "The box room." Once you picked your bed, it was time for inspection. One of the teachers came around with the list of items the school had required us to bring to make sure each of us had everything that we needed. If anything on the list was missing, the school would contact our family to bring the item as soon as possible or the student could be sent home. I had everything on my list. My tuition was paid by my brother directly to the school, including my pocket money for the semester for little items and snacks on campus. When the inspection was completed, we were shown around the other dormitories, then the classrooms, the chapel, the dining hall, the sport's field and the teachers' quarters where all the teachers lived. There were six "Houses" (Dormitories) with different names: Curie, Ibiam, Keller, Montessori, Nightingale and Slessor. I was in Curie

House. There were dormitory heads in each of the Houses who were the final year students, the seniors.

The following day, we were assigned School Sisters. These were the second year students, the class just above us. It was supposed to be a permanent assignment throughout our stay or until our school sisters graduated. They were to guide us, protect us, and help us settle in, since we were the beginners. We were also assigned a School Mother. These were the senior students who were in their fourth or fifth year, and they were to advise us academically. My school mother was a friend to my older sister, Amelia. My school mother and school sister were great people. They were both good to me, yet, I was not interested in social things like that. Some of the new students took the school mother and the school sister thing very seriously. They did assignments with them, did their laundry and some other small chores. Not me. I resented the fact that any student regardless of what year should tell me what to do or ask me to do anything for them. I was very independent, ready and willing to obey the school rules and do whatever the school asked me to do, but I wanted nothing to do with receiving any instructions from a fellow student. I took my studies so seriously that a school mother or sister did not mean much to me; I felt then that they were distractions and not the reason why I was there. Because of this, I abandoned my school mother and school sister. I did not see them that much; neither did I do any chores for them. I was okay, "I do not need any keeper here," I said to myself. I had great classmates; we stuck together because we were the new kids on the block. I finally made a few friends in and outside my class. The friends I had in my class were Atim, Afiong and Dora. We hung together. I appreciated the fact that my school mother and school sister did not pressure me, they just left me alone, and I respected them for that.

We were acclimated to our new environment, sort of, before classes started the following week. We were sixty students and the class was divided into two sections, A and B. Thirty students in each of the classes and we were taking the same courses the first semester. The courses were, English, French, Literature, History, Religion, Geography, Mathematics (Arithmetic, Geometry and Algebra), Home Economics, Biology, Chemistry, Physics and Health Science. In the second semester, there were some changes; the students who passed all the science courses were put in section A to continue doing the science courses as well as Math, English and two other elective courses. Students who did not do well in science courses, were put in section B and they did not take any more science courses. This division of class sections by courses from the second semester remained unchanged until the end of our high school. This had the effect of making the A section of the school look like it had more well-rounded students than the B section. I was in section A and that made me happy because I liked science. We were supposed to choose some of our courses with our future careers in mind. I was clueless then in terms of career choices, so I did not think of any career related courses. I enjoyed Domestic Science because it taught us how to cook, knit, crochet, make things like soaps and lotions and manage a home. As a young girl, I thought at the time that these lessons were going to be handy now and in the future for me as a wife and mother, so, I really liked it. The school was great; it met all my physical, social, spiritual, emotional and intellectual needs. I loved my school!

In the dormitory, the school routine was Monday through Friday, the waking up bell rang at 5:15 AM, lights were turned on and all the students were up, dressed in their sports clothes and down to the field for morning exercise at 5:30 AM, except on rainy days. By 6:00 AM, we were done with exercise, ran to our respective dormitories, took a bath and changed, dressed up in our school uniform and made sure we were in the dining hall at 6:45 AM for breakfast. I took my school bag with me since there was no time for returning to the dormitory after breakfast. From the dining hall, all the students headed to the chapel. Everyone was in her seat according to her grade level by 7:30 AM. There was no lateness allowed and you could not miss Devotion. We would have a twenty-five minute Devotion conducted by the chaplain or one of the teachers. We were done with devotion at 7:55 AM.

Then from the chapel, we went straight to our classes, which started at 8:00 AM. Various courses were taught by different teachers according to their area of specialty until 12:00 noon. We were given a 45-minute class break, where we could do whatever we wanted but be back in class at 12:45 PM. Then school was out for the day by 2:30 PM. We all marched from our respective classes to the dining hall, said our prayers before the meal, then we were served lunch. From the dining hall after lunch, we went back to our dormitories where we changed clothes and got into something comfortable for Siesta at 3:00 PM. Every student in all the dormitories had to be in their beds from 3:00 to 4:00 PM. Then we got up to get ready to go back to the classroom for study time, then called "Prep time," from 4:30 until 6:30 PM. From prep, we went for supper from 6:30-7:00 PM, and we were free to do whatever we wanted to do from after supper until 8:45 PM when the first "Lights out" bell rang in all the dormitories. That meant round up whatever you were doing and get ready for bed. The second "Lights out" bell rang exactly at 9:00 PM and that meant students had to be in their beds and all the lights were turned off for the rest of the night. The Matron made night rounds, to make sure that all the students were accounted for every night after lights out. She would come around with a lantern, checking each bed to make sure we all were in our beds.

An exception was Wednesdays, which were sports' nights so there was no prep time. We had track and field events including the hurdles, javelin, shot put, discus and the short and long jumps. We had our sport practices weekly, and then an inter-house competition was held once a semester. We also had an inter-house music competition every semester.

On Saturdays, we did general cleaning of our dormitories, bathrooms and the surrounding yards from 8:00 to 9:30 AM. Then some of the assigned teachers and the Matron would come for inspection. After the inspection, we would then have what was called, "The Assembly." This was when the principal would address the whole school, then would announce the winning house for the weekly cleaning. Once we were out of the assembly at 10:30 AM, we were free for the rest of the day to do whatever we wanted. On Sundays, we did not have to get up early since we did not have sports in the morning. We could wake up anytime we wanted; we were only required to be in the dining hall by 8:00 AM for breakfast. Then we had to be ready for a church service, at 9:00 AM. We were given a church uniform called "the church white." It was a white and blue flowery dress, with a blue belt and a head tie. It was not a plain white dress, as the name would have suggested it to be. We lined up according to our grades and walked about a mile and a half to the church that was located outside the school grounds in the nearby village. The service was about two hours long. We marched back to school after the church service and then had lunch. We were then free for the rest of the day. However, no student was allowed to go off the school campus without permission and the student had to sign out indicating where they were going, when they would be back and the purpose of their outing. They also had to report and sign in when they came back.

Tuesday evenings were our social nights; we had French club, cultural and dance club, debate society and music club. We had inter-house competitions within the school for the clubs. Sometimes we had weekend socials. Either another secondary school nearby came to our school or we went to theirs for social events. I thought it was a very lively and well-rounded school that would prepare us well for life experience outside the school, in the real world. These were the routines and principles that guided and molded us for four years. My high school taught me the significance of prioritizing, having a sense of direction for what you want, the importance of exercise and activity, time management, spirituality, self-confidence, self-reliance, not yielding to peer pressure, to accept and love yourself for who you are, honesty, respect, integrity, doing your fair share in a group or by yourself, not worrying over what you cannot do anything about, and to have a balanced, contented and happy life. I felt then, that I had no reason not to be successful with such a background.

Then suddenly there was a change in our circumstances. The Nigerian civil war broke out in 1967. All the students had to leave the boarding school to return to their homes. I went home to live in our village with my parents. I was very sad when we were sent away from the school a year before our graduation. I had thought then, that I would be back to complete my high school here after the war, but it did not happen that way. I stayed home in my village with my parents during the war. We were extremely lucky that people in my village did not have to be evacuated. My brother was captured in the city of Calabar, and his wife returned home to my parents with her six children at that time. They stayed with my parents and me until my brother was released from captivity after three months, and he returned to bring his family back to Calabar after the war.

It was the beginning of my senior high school year, when the Nigerian civil war ended. I never went back to the boarding high school. I had to transfer to a different high school closer to home. This had been my second choice high school –Salvation Army Secondary School, Akai, where I had originally interviewed and had been accepted but did not attend. It was a co-educational high school for both boys and girls and I was not used to that. Rather than boarding, I lived at home, walking to and from my new school every day. The school was about thirteen miles from my village. I had to wake up at 4:00 AM and get ready to leave home by 5:00 AM in order to be in school for classes that started at 8:00 AM. Classes ended at 2:00 PM and I would walk the thirteen miles back to get home about 6:30 PM. I would be so tired by the time I got home that all I could do was eat, take a bath and go to bed. Most of the students went through this, since our parents could not now afford the boarding fees so we lived at home. The few students that boarded had to cook for themselves until things got better in the school and at home. I kept up with this rigorous routine for two weeks and it was wearing me out very fast. By the third week, I could again afford the boarding fees; I then had to move into the school and cook for myself like the other students. Then at the end of the first month, the school was able to provide meals to students who could afford it. I continued cooking for myself for three months before I could afford the feeding fees. It was difficult at first, but I had to do the best with what I had. Many students could not even afford to go back to school after the war. I considered myself lucky for what I had. Things got better and normalcy was restored in the school and in the country as a whole. I spent two years in my new school to complete my high school. We had to take the West African qualifying exam, which was equivalent to a high school diploma. The exam passing categories were grade 1, 2, 3 and failure. Grade 1 was the highest passing level; I ended up with grade 2, I was a little disappointed since I was aiming at grade 1.

CHAPTER 7

Life After Secondary (High) School

At that time, it was believed that after high school, finding a good job would be guaranteed since only a few people attended or completed this level of education. Although I had a couple of jobs, probably due to my young age and inexperience, I could not settle into the daily routine of work. Instead, I had this great yearning to continue with my education. I was restless but could not figure out what I wanted to do. All along, I had thought that whatever I had done was to please my parents, I was doing it for them, and it never crossed my mind that I was the one who would benefit from my education and jobs.

I decided to go to college and major in languages. It was at this point that my brother asked me what I wanted to do for a career. I did not understand what he meant by "career" so I told him to give me some time to think about it before giving him an answer. I did not plan to think about it and did not even make any effort to look up the word "career" in the dictionary. That just went over my head. I was clueless. My brother did not get an answer from me, two weeks later; he decided to ask me again. When he posed the question again, I gave him this blank look.

I believe my brother, as a grown man, must have picked up that I had no idea what he was talking about. He gave me a scary look that made me blurt out, "I want to go to college." Then he asked me, "What is going to be your major in college?" "Languages," I replied. He continued, "What career are you going to end up with if your major is going to be in languages?" In my young mind I was saying, "Here we go again with this career stuff." Instead, I said, "That will help me get into the university," "Okay, when you finish from the university what are you going to do for a job?" My brother insisted on an answer. He held me right there, I could not escape. "Hmmm, I do not know yet. Maybe when I finish university, I will have an idea of what I want to do." He gave me such a surprised look and said, "I do not think you are serious nor do I think you know what you are doing. You are very bright in school; I would have imagined that you knew what you wanted to do in life. Since you do not seem to know, I will help you out." He said, "I suggest you go into nursing. It is a good career for women." I was shocked to hear this from my brother. I stood there looking at him like "What are you talking about?" Nevertheless, I dared not asked him that question. I walked away not letting what he just said bother me. I did not know what nurses do. All I thought was that they worked in hospitals and many people died there. This scared me a lot, since I thought that ghosts were in the hospitals all day and night. This was the single reason I would not have anything to do with a hospital. My immediate older sister Alice was a nurse. She used to make me act as her patient in the lab during her free time with her classmates when she was in nursing school. My other sister Amelia worked in the hospital too. I had lived with my two sisters on the hospital premises and never thought of what nurses actually did. I thought I did not like anything to do with the hospital. I kept my fears of the hospital to myself, still not knowing anything else to do other than go back to school.

Meanwhile, my brother looked into the admission process to nursing school. He found out that I would be required to take a federal entrance exam. If I passed, then I would be sent a list of approved nursing schools in the whole country and I could choose where I wanted to attend. Then, I would need to go for the final interview and further exams at the school of my choice. Once my brother had received all the information, he decided to apply for me to the nursing program without ever telling me about it. When the date for the entrance exam was approaching, that was when my brother informed me that he applied for the nursing entrance exam for me. He also stated when and where the exam was going to be held. He told me to be sure I was there fifteen minutes early since I would not be allowed in if I were late. "End of that story, no questions asked, just do it!" he exclaimed. "Yes, I will do it so that you will get off my back," I thought. He had already paid the fee for the exam and had given me some money for spending and for transportation since it involved travelling. I loved travelling, so I agreed to take the exam even though I had already decided not to go to the nursing school if I passed.

I was thrilled as the date was approaching; I started counting down the days until the date for the nursing school entrance exam finally came. I travelled by a bus for a couple of hours to the exam center and reluctantly went into the exam hall. There were proctors everywhere since there were many candidates. As I walked into the exam hall, there was a list with all the candidates' names on it, arranged in alphabetical order with an assigned number beside each name. These numbers were our seating order; they were also written on our seats. When we walked in, we were asked our full name and it was checked off the list. Then, we were escorted to our seats. We were provided with test papers and pencils. The instructions were read aloud thus: "No personal belongings on your desk, no talking or any form of distraction, do not get up until you are done. When you are done, put up your hand and a proctor will come to your seat to collect your test papers and pencils. Walk out quietly when you are done knowing that others will still be taking the exams." The exams were distributed to each candidate after the instructions were read. They were multiple-choice questions. There were 100 questions for one and a half hours, starting at 9:00 AM. Once we started, the entrance door was locked so that no one who was late could come in. The test results were going to be sent both to us and to the nursing school of our choice.

I was noisy to the point that the two candidates who sat on either side of me moved further away. Thinking back on this, I am surprised that I was not dismissed from the exam hall for causing a distraction. I must have finished when about 2/3 of the people were done. My exam papers were collected, and then I left, not worrying or giving a thought to the test I just took. I did not care about how I did. I was just happy that it was over and had prayed that I would fail the exam. One of the candidates who sat beside me had taken this exam before and failed. This was her second attempt. She had one more chance since you had three attempts and then you were out if you did not make it the third time. I felt bad for her because she really wanted to be a nurse and she could not go into an approved nursing program without passing this exam. I went shopping after the exam and bought whatever I could with the amount of money I had before heading back home. I enjoyed the shopping and the travelling and totally blocked out of my mind that I had just taken an entrance exam to go into a nursing school.

After the nursing school exam, I went home to my parents and was trying to figure out what I was now going to do. I started applying for other jobs. I obtained my first job as a teacher in a primary school, teaching third graders. My uncle on my maternal side was the Headmaster of the school. He was "on my case" because he felt that as a woman, at my age (twenty), I was not shy, I was too bold, I laughed a lot and too loud and he said he felt bad for my mother (who was his stepsister) for having a daughter like me because I was not going to amount to anything in the future. I thought, "I do not need this from anybody!" I had been abused as a child in my brother's house, and once I survived that, I became extremely reactive to any form of tone, attitude or action that reminded me of that oppression. I had vowed to stand up for myself for the rest of my life. I knew then that this job was not going to work out with my uncle. I loved the students, but I had to get out of there quick! At the end of the month, I went home to my parents and never went back to the school. That was it for me with this job, I quit!

After the teaching experience, I decided to go back to my brother's house since he was living in the big city, to look for a job there. By this time, he had already transferred from the North back to Calabar in Cross River State. My brother always seemed like a father to me because of the age differ-ence and his children were like my siblings since I had lived with them all of their lives until I left for high school. When I went back to them after high school, the children, now six of them, were very happy to see me and I was happy to see them too. My brothers' children respected me like their big sister rather than their aunt and wanted to be around me. I was now like a role model for them. They loved me and I loved them in return. I bought gifts for them since now I could afford it. This was awesome. I thought, "I am grown up now, and my brother's wife is going to treat me with respect." I was wrong. She was observing my interaction with her children and she was not pleased. She was so upset that she started accusing me of spoiling her children, she felt that her children were not listening to her or having any regard for her since I had come back; they were now clinging to me. Here we go again! When I had left her house for high school, I had forgiven her for all the abuse I suffered from her. I had gained my freedom, and I was moving on. However, when I returned to her house after high school while trying to figure out where fate was taking me, she started to abuse me terribly again, verbally and emotionally.

On one of these abusive occasions, I had planned to visit our oldest sister who was sick in a nearby hospital in Calabar. I bought her some bananas and oranges and then plucked six guavas from the tree, which grew behind my brother's house, to bring to her. When I returned from the hospital, my brother's wife started yelling about the fact that I had plucked some guavas. She made so much noise about it but I never said anything to her. I kept in my room to avoid any confrontation with her. When my brother came back from work that day, his wife told him how I had plucked the guavas without her permission and said, "How dare she touch my guavas!" I kept to my room and the children were with me most of the time.

My brother did not say anything to me. Then at 3:00 AM that night, he woke me up and asked me to come to the living room because he wanted to talk to me. I had said my prayers and I was in peace. I would not let what he was going to say bother me. I had asked the Lord to give me His grace once more to make it through in my brother's house. It did not matter to me what my brother or his wife were going to say or do, making a big deal about six guavas when the guava tree was full of fruits and she was not the person who planted it. The guava tree was already there when they moved into this government quarters. My brother started by asking me why I had plucked the guavas. I did not answer him. He continued talking by belittling me, saying he thought that I was grown up enough to know better, not to touch anything in his house or yard without his wife's permission. He continued saying that I was having a bad influence on his children. He went on and on! I became very hardened, looking straight into my brother's face without saying a word. It was very painful to me for my brother and his wife to be that concerned about the guavas and not about our dear sister who was seriously ill in the hospital. When my brother was done talking, he said to me, "Get out of my face, I am ashamed that you've not shown any maturity at your age. You are still behaving like these children." Still stone-faced, I walked away back to my room, shut the door and then I lost it. I cried inconsolably. It was too painful to me how my brother and his wife had no sympathy for our sister who was very ill. Both my brother and his wife were so unreasonable and hardhearted to be whining over six guavas. I was upset to the point that all the past horrible experiences I had at my brother's house came flashing back. It was hard and I was very angry! This incident took place on a Thursday. It was so painful and overwhelming that the endless tears continued to flow from my eyes, I could not eat for four days and I was really down. I did all the chores without a word to anybody in the house. I felt bad for the children; they tried, but could not lift my spirits so they left me alone. On the third day of my not eating, my brother's wife told him that I had not eaten for the past three days and so my brother came to tell me that if I did not eat immediately, he was going to send me to my parents in the village. Whatever he said did not matter to me. All that crossed my mind now was, if I did not get out of my brother's house soon, it was going to be worse than when I was younger and there was no way I could handle that now. On the fourth day still not eating, I had lost a lot of weight; I decided to take my few belongings and return home to my parents in the village. I prayed to the Lord never to stay again at my brother's house if it was possible. I thought that I may visit, but that's all. Other decisions I made that day were:

(1)   Never to eat any fruit in my brother's house.
(2)   To stay away from my brother and his wife as much as I could.
(3)   To find my way in life so that I did not ever have to go through the agony of my brother's wife's abuse in any form, for the rest of my life.

When I returned to my parents in our village, I did not tell my mother what had happened. She noticed and commented that I had lost a lot of weight and asked if I was sick. "No, I am okay," I said. She was worried and seemed not to believe that I was all right, so she said, "You can tell me what is bothering you whenever you want." In my mind, there was nothing to talk about. I was now older and as a young adult, I had to handle my own problems.

CHAPTER 8

My First "Real" Job

Finally, I was hired by the Ministry of Agriculture as a payroll clerk in Calabar, the city my brother was living in. I was thrilled about this but now I had to go back to my brother's house. My plan was to stay there only until I had enough money to move out to my own apartment. Two weeks after I started working, I noticed that this new job was very boring to me; I was disheartened by the thought that someone could do this for the rest of his or her life. I saw older people that had been there for years. I was given a table with an adding machine, some papers and pens. Each department would send in the hours worked and the pay rate of their employees. It was our responsibility to calculate their pay, deduct their taxes and other deductibles and then send the pay voucher to Accounts Payable for the employees to be paid at the end of each month. Three of us were hired on the same day right out of high school and the manager of our department had warned us that if we quit we were going to pay certain penalties. I thought to myself that this was just to threaten us to stay; probably they had a high turnover from high school graduates.

I worked for two months, and when my first paycheck came, I was surprised to be paid so much! This made me happy but not enough to settle down in what I considered this boring job. I still had this strong inclination to go back to school. I divided my first pay into three. I gave a portion to my mother, a portion to my immediate older sister Alice and kept the rest for myself. My brother had expected me to bring my first paycheck to him and I did not. He noticed that I had shopped, bought clothes and shoes and I had started dressing better. I kept the remaining money under my bed. I did not know enough to open an account in the bank then. My brother asked me if I was paid and I said yes. He said, "You started spending the money without showing it to me to bless your first pay?" "Yes," I said, "I did not need to show it to you, I earned it." That did not go well with him. He was angry, but I was not bothered by his reaction. I thought, "He would have taken all the money from me if I had shown it to him."

It was just at this time, the result of the entrance exam for the nursing school was mailed to me. To my surprise, I passed. With the exam result was the date and time for the interview for the nursing school of my choice. I was now happy that I passed even though I had prayed against it. At least, it would get me out of my brother's house sooner. I had purposely chosen a nursing school in a different state, the North, far from home, even though there were nursing schools nearby, so that I could escape from my home and travel there for the interview.

I had made it very clear that I did not like nursing. When the time for the interview drew near, I needed to request some time off from work. I did not have enough money to pay my way, so I asked my brother for help. He refused to help me because I chose a school so far away and because I had said I did not like nursing. He said he was not going to waste his hard-earned money on me anymore. I went to my older sister Amelia and asked her for help. She was happy and willing to sponsor me provided I promised to go to the nursing school if I passed the interview. She said if I passed the interview and then attended the school, that would be all right, but if I passed the interview and refused to go to the school, I would have to refund to her all the money she had given me. "Deal," I said, although in my mind I was still not planning to go to the nursing school.

I packed my little suitcase and was seen off by my sister Amelia at the transportation station. It was a rough lorry ride on dusty untarred roads for three days. The driver stopped at a couple of gas stations for food and bathroom breaks. By the time we arrived at Zaria in the North, I was covered with layers of red dust; I started coughing, most likely from inhalation of the dusty air. I could not wait to take a bath, brush my teeth, freshen up and get something to eat. My interview was the following day, so I had one day to rest and recuperate from the tedious journey and then looked around the university campus. The prospective students were given a place to stay on campus and we were fed. The nursing school was at Ahmadu Bello University. It was a big university hospital school of nursing in Zaria, Nigeria. I was happy that I made it all that distance.

On the day of the exam and interview, we were taken to a large classroom where the testing took place. We were given two types of exams, a multiple choice and then two essay exams. We were supposed to fill in all the questions on the multiple choice exam. On the essay exam, we were given five topics and had to choose two questions to write on. All the candidates had to do the # 1 essay, which was, "Why do I want to be a nurse?" The second choice, which I picked to write about, was called, "Trying to fit a square peg in a round hole." For me, the second topic required imagination; the first topic was more straightforward. When we were done with the written exam, we were sent to another room for an oral interview. I was in a room with one interviewer. To my surprise, the question of why I wanted to be a nurse came up again. I thought, "they really want to select candidates that are serious that's why they were asking this question again during the oral interview." I told my interviewer that I had two older sisters who were nurses and they inspired me. I had seen them at work, visited them all the time and I couldn't wait to join them in this noble profession. I did not lack words or the imagination to make the interviewer believe me. I had a strong conviction that I was going to be accepted after this interview. If so, what was I going to do? I still did not want to be a nurse. However, there was no need worrying about this now. I enjoyed my travelling experience and that was all I wanted. Mission accomplished!

I was finished with the exams and the interviews and ready to go back home to my brother's house on the third day. I got there safely and went back to work while still living with my brother. Three weeks later, the nursing school exam and interview results came out and I passed. I was happy. Passing an exam always made me feel good. Now I was gripped by the reality that I was toying with what I feared the most- the idea of going to a nursing school and now I could actually end up going to this school. Oh no! Not me! Here I was again, struggling with myself. Enclosed with the exam's result was the date the nursing school was going to start. They requested an acceptance letter from me to assure them that I was coming, and I was to arrive three days before classes started. I did not do any of what the nursing school had requested.

A week after the school had started I received a reminder from the nursing school in the mail saying they had reserved a place for me; they were worried about where I was or if something had happened to me. The school needed to hear from me. I talked to my sister Amelia and she advised me to contact the school right away to let them know that I was coming. She said, "Do not miss this opportunity, it is a great profession." I said to my sister, "For real, do I have to go? I do not like nursing." "Yes," she replied, "do not waste any more time." "Okay!" I said angrily, to my sister. I had continued working at my other job, as I was getting ready to leave for the nursing school. I was still somewhat new at work and never told my co-workers what was going on in my life. I went home to my village that weekend to tell my parents about my new adventure and to say goodbye to my family. Then I came back to my brother's house in Calabar on Sunday evening, to get ready to leave on Monday. I decided to call out sick from work on that Monday when I left for nursing school and I never heard anything from work again. They probably had no idea what happened to me. I had to say goodbye to my brother and his family. I was so attached to his children, it made it hard to say goodbye. We hugged and cried; the youngest one then was about two years old. He broke my heart, since he was too little to talk then, yet I felt his love for me. As hard as it was to let go of the children, I finally had to leave. My sister Amelia who came to see me off gave me some money and went with me to the transportation station.

CHAPTER 9

Going to Nursing School

I finally arrived late at Wusasa Hospital School of Nursing in Zaria where I was told that it was a part of the Ahmadu Bello University School of Nursing Program. It was already the second week of school when I joined my class and my Nursing Instructor was so happy that I finally made it. For an unknown reason to me, she never bothered to ask why I did not arrive earlier. I thanked God for her not asking because her pushing on that would have just sent me packing right back home before I had even started. My Nursing Instructor was a British woman by the name of Sister Wright, and she was a very kind and understanding person. She did not make a big deal about my late arrival.

There were thirty nursing students in class, twenty-eight women and two men. Nursing then, seemed to be seen as a profession mostly dominated by women. The nursing programs were hospital- based so the students lived on the hospital premises. The men and women lived in separate living quarters but shared both the dining hall and the Chapel. There were five students from my state - the then Cross River State, and the rest of the students came from other states in Nigeria. There were two or three students in each dormitory room. Some of our roommates were also our classmates and some were not. My roommate was my classmate although she was from a different state, and she spoke a different language. We got along well together and became close friends.

At the beginning of my journey as a "nurse-to-be," I was made to understand that the first three months of the program we were going to be in the classroom for these classes: Introduction to Nursing, Nursing Principles and Theories, Anatomy and Physiology, Pharmacology, Medication Calculations and Pathophysiology. The courses I took in high school were very helpful: English, French, Math, Chemistry, Biology, Physics, Health Science and Geography. I had no idea while I was taking those high school courses that they were going to be so helpful to me in the future. The subject matter was not new to me but now was being taught in more detail. I did well in class and in my exams. Since I had never failed any exam to this point, it gave me the confidence to think that an exam was a means to propel me forward for success. I had never had exam anxieties but I also made sure I studied enough to walk into the exam hall confidently.

During the first three-month period of being in nursing school, we had classes and labs only. We had nothing to do with the hospital units where the patients were cared for. I had thought at this point that nursing was only the academic aspect. I was settling in without any problem. Things were going okay; most importantly to me, I had not seen any ghosts around. Since I was a little girl, I had always been afraid of hospitals because I thought that ghosts were all over the place since many people died there.

Following our first three months in class, we were supposed to be gradually introduced to the hospital units. In those days, hospitals were separated into male and female units. On our first day, Sister Wright took us to a female medical unit. I was so scared that I was going to catch a disease just by breathing in the hospital air. The patients had all kinds of diseases and I still thought that germs were floating invisibly on the patients' bodies and in the hospital units. For this reason, I stood at the entrance to the unit with my arms folded across my chest, making sure I did not touch anything. All my classmates had followed Sister Wright, who was our Clinical Instructor, into the hospital unit. They were saying hello to the patients in their beds as my Clinical Instructor introduced them as the new nursing students.

When we left the unit, Sister Wright took us to a room where dirty equipment and soiled linens were kept until they were cleaned, called the "sluice room" at the time. There were some linens soiled with blood soaking in the sink. She dipped her hands into this bloody sink and started rinsing the linen out. As she was doing this, she was talking to us saying, "You do not send soiled linen to the laundry room. Whether it is soiled with blood or feces, you have to rinse them out first."

During that era, that was what we used to do. At this point, I stood there shocked that she just put her hands into that mess without gloves. Even if she had gloves on, it still grossed me out! Now I was thinking, "Is this what I would be expected to do as a nurse? God forbid!" I decided then that I had enough of nursing, I thought; and "I am out of here!" We were given a half-hour break after we left the patients' unit, to return to the class to discuss what we had observed on the hospital unit we had just visited. I had nothing to say since I had already made my final decision to leave. Other students talked about what they observed and what they understood from their observations. Sister Wright explained much of the details of what we saw in order for it to make more sense to us.

I went back to my room after school that day and packed my suitcase, ready to go back home immediately. I could not take it anymore. That evening I went to tell Sister Wright that I was leaving the following day because nursing was not for me and I have never had liked it. It was then that I told her why I was late for the two weeks; I confessed to her the whole truth. I told her how my brother had applied to the school for me and had forced me into going to school for nursing. "I do not like it and I am very scared of ghosts, which hounds the hospital premises. They will kill me one day. Please, I want to go home tomorrow." Sister Wright was shocked to hear what I was saying and said to me, "I know that you are very young. You do not understand what nursing is all about. I want you to stay here for the next three months. By then you will understand a lot better and can make a well-informed decision. If I let you go now, even God in heaven would hold me accountable and you have no basis to make such a crucial decision now. I can see you making a wonderful, caring nurse in the future. I just cannot let you go at this time." She then asked me, "Have you paid your tuition?" "No," I said, crying frantically, because I never expected that she would object to my leaving. "I kept my tuition to pay my way back home," and she asked me where I kept the money. I told her at the right hand corner of my suitcase on my nightstand. Sister Wright hugged me and started praying while still holding unto me. After her prayers, she let go of me and I walked away to my room, still crying. I was so lost in my disappointment, anger and frustration. As I jumped into my bed, I heard a knock on my unlocked door and I did not respond to it. It was Sister Wright coming to get the money for safekeeping. She opened the unlocked door and without a word to me, opened my suitcase, took the money from the right-hand side of the suitcase and left the room. That was all the money I had. This would mean no going back home for me!

I felt I could not go back to classes for the rest of that week, which was three school days. I cried all the time, I did not want to be there anymore, and I was very depressed. I was in bed most of the time. Since I was not attending classes, some of the students thought I was sick. After school each day, Sister Wright would come and check on me; sometimes she would take me out. She tried as much as she could to cheer me up and to convince me to stay. I do not think that even my mother would have had this kind of patience with me, but Sister Wright did.

The following week I went back to class sadly. Sister Wright kept looking out for me until I fully recovered. There were schedules made for us as we started learning in different areas. We were in the classroom on Monday, Wednesday and Friday, labs were on Tuesday and clinical practice in the hospital was on Thursday. We were free on weekends. This was how it was for the next three months. I started getting used to the hospital units and although I was still watching out for ghosts, I never saw any and did not see or hear of any patient who died in the hospital while I was there. On our clinical days, we were started with instructions on learning to talk to patients, then taking health histories, bed making, taking vital signs, bathing, feeding and calculation of fluid intake and output. We were taught these skills in class and then practiced them in the lab before we attempted them in the clinical areas in the hospital, always with assistance until we were comfortable doing them independently. Our Clinical Instructor, Sister Wright, was always on the hospital unit with us and she and the senior students were very helpful.

It was on one of the clinical days in the hospital that I helped a senior student admit a patient by the name of Hawa. She was a 45-year-old patient, who came in with a diagnosis of congestive cardiac (heart) failure. She had bilateral pedal edema (which was the swelling of both lower legs) and shortness of breath. She was in bed with the head of her bed up to help her breathe a little easier and she was on oxygen via the nasal cannula (a tube used to connect oxygen from the tank or source to the patient). I could see that she was struggling to breathe.

I felt so bad for Hawa that I would have done anything for her to make her feel better. I was very attentive to Hawa and I prayed that she would feel better. Each morning, even when we were not having clinical that day, I still ran to the hospital unit to see how Hawa was doing. Luckily for me, each time I visited, she was getting better. On the fifth day, she was strong enough to get out of bed and go to the bathroom by herself without any oxygen and she was not out of breath. I was thrilled.

That day after school, I went back to the hospital floor to give her a shower, I also fixed her hair, and she looked so much better. I was ecstatic. This was the first time "I got it," the "Ah-Ha Moment" on what it meant to be a nurse—helping people who are sick to regain their health and independence. It was a revelation for me.

This is why I will never forget Hawa. I still remember her face very clearly. She was the patient that made a turning point in my life as a nurse-to-be. From then on, I poured out my whole being into helping the sick. During my free time, I would go to the hospital unit to help with whatever I could do for the patients.

At the end of the six months, we had to take a comprehensive examination called the "Prelim." This exam was to determine our fate of whether we were going to progress in the nursing program or not. At the time, if you passed the exam, were of good behavior, had moral character and a caring attitude, you were guaranteed to go on. If you did not have these attributes and you passed the exam, you were advised on other career choices and would be sent away from the nursing school. It was felt then that you would not become a good nurse. However, if you had the required attributes but failed the exam, you would then be allowed to stay and repeat the class. We took the exam and the day the results were out, Sister Wright decided to call us individually into her office to give us our results. We all gathered in front of her office nervously. We were called in by alphabetical order according to our last names. I was the last student to be called in since my last name started with a U. When a student went in and came out happy, rejoicing and smiling, we who were waiting outside assumed that the student was successful. If any student came out crying, and sad, then we thought that either they had failed or were being sent away because of their character. Some of the students, whether they passed or failed, hung around to find out the fate of the other students while a few of them left.

I went in last and Sister Wright said, "Hi Enoh. You did very well. Congratulations. I knew you would do well and I still maintain that you will make a good nurse. Now let us pray first before you respond to my question, if you've changed your mind to stay in the nursing program or you still want to leave." I knelt down with quiet tears running down my cheeks. She prayed and after the prayer Sister Wright said to me, "I will not hold you back whatever your decision is today. You've had some experience that should help you make an informed decision by now." I stood up, gave her a big hug and said to her "Sister, I thank you and my brother and I give God the glory, for it was meant to be. I tried with all my might to run away from God's call but wherever I ran to, God turned me back. It is now that I understand why. I promise you by the grace of the Lord that I will remain a Nurse for the rest of my life. This was not my first choice, but I believe it is God's choice for me. I believe you and I believe now in myself that God is going to make me become a great nurse. He has called me and I have answered. Thank you for both your guidance and your patience with me." Then Sister Wright blessed me and I left her office, humbled, in tears, as if I had a divine encounter.

I did not say anything to my classmates that were waiting outside for me. I went straight to my room, continuing to give thanks to the Lord and crying. The students waiting and watching for me to come out of the office, saw me crying and thought I had failed. They all expected me to be leaving but I was not going anywhere. None of my classmates were willing to ask me what happened and I did not tell anyone of my encounter with Sister Wright until years after I was done with the nursing program. For me this was a moment to be cherished for the rest of my life. It was a turning point for me, when I said "Yes" to the Lord and was ready and willing to carry out His will for me as a Nurse. It was a moment that changed the course of my life. I was now focused, I had a sense of direction, and I had peace within me. I was no more fighting within myself and with the world around me about my future. I had my future in sight at last. I will be a Nurse!

CHAPTER 10

A Student Nurse "For Real"

The confirmation of my life's destiny gave me a new zeal. I plunged my whole being into my nursing schoolwork and taking care of my patients both when I was on and off duty. I would walk to the patient unit and offer to help with anything I could do. Our dormitory was on the school premises, so it was a walking distance to the hospital. After the comprehensive (preliminary) exam, we were now officially known to be "Student Nurses." Those of us that met all the requirements were kept on to continue in the nursing program. We started working more on the hospital unit as First Year Nursing Students.

Our routine was to work a full 8-hour shift either days or evenings. There were no nights assigned to us at this stage. We worked three days a week including alternate weekends. We were now allowed to make beds, bathe and feed the patients, take vital signs, do fluid intake and output, empty bedside drainage and help with the admission of patients to the hospital unit. We still had classes on Mondays, Wednesdays and Fridays and one lab a week. We were given a detailed schedule so we knew where to be and what to do at all times.

In our second year of the Nursing Program, we were introduced to medication administration as well as dressing changes and total patient care. The more days we spent on the clinical site in the hospital, the less time we had for our routine academics. Now our learning was taking place in class, in the lab and on the clinical units at the hospital. It was a great teaching method; it made more sense to transfer what we learned in classes and labs to "hands- on" in the clinical units. We were rotated to all the nursing units in the hospital, which then included the male medical/surgical units, the female medical/surgical units, orthopedic, pediatrics, maternity, emergency room (ER), operating room (OR) and public health, which was going out into the community. I loved it all and I was very happy. By the third year, we were going to be senior nursing students and we were helping on the hospital units, doing everything with one Registered Nurse (RN) as the unit manager. It felt so good; I already felt like a nurse, but I was not licensed yet. By the end of the third year, we were preparing to take our final school exam. If we passed, then we were eligible for the National Certifying Nursing Exam. As we worked and attended classes, we had been taking exams all along. If we failed any of the classes, we had to repeat them because a certain level of knowledge is necessary to be a competent nurse. We took exams in every area that was covered in class. It was not easy at times, but I found it very fulfilling and exciting even with the rigor of the program.

My first experience of a patient death was in my second year in nursing school. It was one of my patients who died. She was admitted that day with a diagnosis of multi-organ failure. She was very sick and had difficulty breathing. This patient kept asking for a bedpan frequently but was unable to pass any urine or stool. Finally, the RN that was on duty with me said, "Do not put that patient anymore on the bedpan, stay with her and observe her breathing, she could go any minute from now." I went back to count this patient's respirations and she took a long gasp and that was it. I stood there looking at my patient without understanding that this was her last breath. The RN who was observing the patient with me said, "That's it, she is gone." The RN asked me to pull the screen for privacy for this patient; she then put this patient's head of bed down, laying her flat on her back. When we left this patient's bedside to go back to the nurse's station, the RN told me that my patient was dead and she now had to call the doctor to come and pronounce the body as deceased. This happened at 8:00 PM. I was so scared I could not move. I stood frozen at that nurse's station until 9:00 PM, which was the end of my shift. The doctor came and pronounced the body, post mortem care was done and the body was taken to the mortuary. I still felt I could not move from where I stood. Finally, I had to leave since my shift was over. I was so afraid, I had to ask a friend to escort me to my dormitory and I could not sleep alone for two weeks. I kept looking out for this patient's ghost day and night, but I never saw any. I started dispelling myself of the intense unfounded fear of ghosts that I had all my life. "Maybe there are no ghosts," I thought. I have never seen one, in spite of dealing with deaths as a nurse. I would now be free of the fear of ghosts!

Being born into a Christian family, protestant by religion, I had gone to church on Sundays with my parents and with my brother when I lived with him. It was just a routine then and I never thought of what it meant to be a Christian until I finished high school. It was then that I realized that just going to church does not make you a Christian. I started seeking the truth. I explored other religions and attended different churches. My mother was worried and concerned over what I was going through. I assured her that I was looking for the truth. I understood then that this is what I had to do for myself; nobody could do it for me.

I was in this mode of truth seeking when I left for nursing school. At my nursing school, they had Scripture Union (SU) where a group of Christians had religious meetings and prayers weekly. I never attended these meetings at first. Some of the members invited me many times to join them, but I declined. I finally decided to check it out after a couple of months in school. I attended the meetings many times with no impact. Then on one particular evening, it was a fasting and prayer meeting. As we prayed and praised the Lord, I had a divine encounter, and since then, I realized the truth I was seeking. I yielded to the Lord and my life changed forever.

The Lord had always been with me all along but I did not really understand until that day.

Now that I had found the truth that I was seeking, I believed, trusted and leaned completely on the Lord. He has never disappointed me even when I do not understand what is happening. He has done numerous miracles on a daily basis for me. Nothing is too small or too big for the Lord. Even when I mess up, He still sees me through successfully. The Lord has given me inner peace, joy, happiness and contentment that radiates in my personality. I am an optimist. I see something good in all situations and all my cups are half-full. I always try to put a smile on my patient's face as sick as they may be.

I finally completed the nursing program successfully, earning my RN (Registered Nurse) certificate and then working for nine months in the same hospital. Those of us who elected to stay and work for this hospital were moved from the nursing school dormitory to the staff living quarters also on the hospital premises. Those who wanted to leave to work in other hospitals were free to go. For the three and a half years we were there as students, the hospital was paying us some money as a stipend. We thought that was all we would receive. We were surprised when we were paid a lump sum of money at the completion of the nursing program. For me, it was a lot of money. We were paid in cash and I had never handled that much money in my life. Some of my counterparts counted their money right there. I did not count mine immediately. Instead, I took the money to my room thanking God for His unexpected blessing. I then used this money to open my very first bank account. This lump sum of money also helped me with my expenses to start out in real life as an adult.

While still working at the nursing school hospital as a registered nurse (RN), I was applying to Midwifery school in my home state, then called Cross River State, in Nigeria. I wanted to go back home to be closer to my parents since they were getting older and I was so far from them. At that time, Midwifery school was only a year if you already had your RN. In Nigeria then, when you had both your RN and Midwifery, you were considered to be "double qualified." Some people only had one or the other, which was okay in terms of job opportunity. I wanted to go to Midwifery school because I felt it would make me feel more complete as a nurse and I would have better job opportunities and be free to explore any nursing area I would want to specialize in. I was informed that my state of origin, Cross River State would not accept me back from the North without an interstate transfer through the Ministry of Health. I was surprised and upset at this, but not wanting to lose the entrance time, I decided to apply to a school of midwifery in a state closer to home called, Imo State and I was accepted at Ramat Specialist Hospital, Umuahia, thank God. It was closer to home, a four hour drive instead of the three days it took me to get to the North. I took some time off to spend with my parents before Midwifery school started. It was nice to have some downtime. My Mom was very happy for me and pleased with my career progress.

Arriving three months early at Ramat Specialist Hospital, Umuahia, in Imo State, I started working on a male surgical unit as an RN. From my name and accent, the patients and the staff on the unit knew my state of origin. What they could not figure out was whether I understood and spoke their language, Ibo, or not. One day on duty, a couple of the patients were debating about this, so they decided to say some funny cuss words to see my reaction. Since I understood Ibo, which was their language, I made a conscious decision not to react to whatever they were going to say. To avoid betraying myself, I decided to fix my gaze on a specific spot and stay focused to avoid laughing. They said a couple of very funny things and were laughing so hard. I totally acted as if I did not understand them. Therefore, they concluded that I did not understand their language. The patients made sure everybody on that unit thought that I did not understand them. I waited for a couple of minutes, and then stepped off the floor to go outside and laugh. It was so funny and I did not know how I was going to come back to the floor with a straight face to deal with these patients. I came back and went straight to the medication room to recollect myself before I went back to take care of my patients. Before you know it, everyone around the hospital thought that I did not understand Ibo. I did not disclose to them that I understood and spoke Ibo fluently. It was in the Midwifery school that I surprised my friends with how fluent I was in their language.

Now at the Midwifery school, we lived on the hospital premises in a dormitory, two students to a room. We were housed and fed by the hospital. I made many friends and my Midwifery school experience was awesome. When I had been in the nursing school program, we did touch on maternity nursing and clinical practice but it was not as detailed as it was in the Midwifery school. We had classes the first three months and in the fourth month, labs and clinical practice were added to our schedule. Then in the sixth month, we were fully working on the maternity units and attending classes. The maternity units were divided into:

(1) Prenatal clinics where women registered in the early stages of their pregnancy and received prenatal care. They received prenatal vitamins and were monitored for vital signs, weight, and fundal height (how big a pregnant belly is according to the gestational age.) Fetal (baby's) heart rate and the general health of the women were also checked. Labs were done including urine testing. As the pregnancy advanced, the frequency of the clinic visits increased.

(2) Ante-partum for women whose pregnancies were advanced but they were not due for delivery and they still had health issues.

(3) Peri-partum period, made up of patients that were due for delivery, maybe in active labor or for induction.

(4) Labor and delivery (L&D). Here, the pregnant patient's delivery was imminent and delivery took place in this section.

(5) Post-partum, for patients that had delivered and were transferred from L&D to this unit for post-partum care.

(6)   The newborn nursery, where the babies were kept, and were taken to their mothers for breast-feeding only. The newborn nursery nurse took care of all the babies.

We were twenty-five students in our class, divided into each of the sections and were rotated so that each of the students had the opportunity to work in each of these areas.

We were given class exams as we went along. At the end of one year, we took our final written midwifery school and the national midwifery exam. If we did not pass the midwifery school exam, we were not allowed to take the national exam. I passed both exams and then worked on the same unit as a Registered Midwife in order to gain more experience and self-confidence. Of all the divisions in maternity, I loved and enjoyed working in the newborn nursery the most. Labor and delivery was a good experience for me but the women were in a lot of pain, which made me sad until the baby was born. The miracle of birth is inexplicable. It is phenomenal to witness the delivery of a healthy newborn baby. The mother and all the family members and friends are very happy. The health care team members are excited. It is always a good feeling all around. It is very sad when a patient delivers an abnormal or stillborn baby. The intense sadness and grief is shared by the patient, families, friends and the health care team. I witnessed the delivery of an anencephalic baby, (a baby without the top of the head). He had all the facial features. It was awful and the baby boy was alive. The parents were crying and we were very sad too. The prenatal clinic was okay, there was nothing too exciting for me in that department except the first time I heard a fetal heartbeat, which was amazing! I did not prefer the post-partum unit then.

When I felt comfortable with maternity nursing, I was offered a position in the Operating Room (OR), in the same hospital. This made me nervous at first but with a good orientation, I became more comfortable. OR nursing is very different. There are specific protocols, for example, scrubbing for the sterile procedure, putting on (downing) of sterile gowns, gloves and masks, getting the patient ready for the procedure, setting up the right instruments for the specific type of surgery, counting of all the instruments and swabs both before and after surgery and the induction of anesthesia by the anesthesiologist and the patient protocol. I was trained as a runner, who was an RN, responsible for the smooth running of the OR during a surgical procedure. The role of the Surgical Assistant was to assist the Surgeon during surgery. Then, there was an Instrument Nurse. Their responsibility was to hand the surgeon the right sterile instrument when the Surgeon asked for it. You have to know what instruments are used in any type of surgery. When I started working in the OR, I kept wondering when I would ever learn all these instruments. In retrospect, that was what scared me the most. I refused to quit, I kept going. Eventually before I knew it, I understood. Once "I got it," I fell in love with OR nursing. It was a very different culture and environment within the hospital. This was the only OR in this hospital and all kinds of surgeries were performed here. We had a surgical list for each day. When the scheduled surgeries were all done, and on weekends, some of the surgical teams were put on call for emergencies. I missed certain aspects of the floor or unit nursing where we had a longer period to spend with the patients. In OR nursing you had only minutes to spend with the patients while they were awake. The rest of the time the patient is in the OR, they may be unconscious under anesthesia. We still cared for them during their surgery. I really, really loved OR Nursing once I learned what I was doing. I worked there for about two years but the burning desire for higher education would not let me settle there, and I felt I had to move on.

CHAPTER 11

Plans to Go to America

I t was earlier, during my psychiatric rotation in the nursing school program at Ahmadu Bello University in Kaduna, Nigeria, that I met my nephew (my senior sister's oldest son) for the very first time. He was raised outside my village in one of the big cities. He had come from Lagos in the West, to Kaduna in the North to obtain a visa to go to America. This was the first time the dream of going to America was introduced to me. During that meeting, I expressed my interest in joining him in America in the future, when I was done with midwifery school. He said to me, "Enoh, it would be a good idea for you to come to America, but since you are a woman, you may find a man tomorrow and decide to marry and settle down, forgetting all about 'coming to America'." I said to him, "I do not think so. You are talking to a strong woman, and a man is not the foremost thing on my mind right now. I want to get a good education so that I can end up in good jobs;

this is my first priority before a husband." I told him that, "If I start out well, then every part of my life would fall into place, that's how I feel." I thought, "After having such a rough childhood, I do not ever want to be dependent on anybody." I had learned early in life that depending on other people robs you of your true freedom and independence. "Right now, I am striving to pave the way for myself that leads to total freedom. I do not mind people depending on me; but never again will I be dependent on anybody except God." I had heard and studied about America earlier in school. Going to America never occurred to me until after that meeting with my nephew. This was the birth of my dream, going to America.

This conversation with my nephew brought new hopes and opened new doors of opportunity that I had never imagined. New dreams, "I will be going to America when I am done with midwifery school." I was very certain about this. I believed it and started acting on my belief. My nephew obtained his visa and left for America. Once I completed nursing school, which was three and a half years, one year of midwifery school was like a breeze and a good stepping-stone for me. While in midwifery school, I started making plans for leaving to America. I started applying to several schools in different states in the U.S. Some of the schools requested exams such as the TOEFL, SAT and ACT. Not knowing what these names of tests meant but wanting to leave my country for America so bad, I took them all. When I took the TOEFL, the huge hall was filled with other candidates taking the same exam. When I went in to take the ACT and SAT,

I was expecting many candidates too, only to find out that I was the only one. For both of the exams I had different dates and testing centers. I was taken to a small quiet room by the person who would be proctoring the exam. He gave me the testing materials, told me the time allocated for the test and left, checking on me from time to time. All the exam materials were collected from me once I was done. With TOEFL, several people proctored the exam. They had a list with the candidates' names and numbers that they had to check off both before and after the exam. This written exam was timed too. I was told that when the results for the three exams were out, they were going to be sent to the schools I had applied to, in the U.S and a copy to me. I received my test results but did not know how to interpret them. I had hoped that I did well enough to gain an admission into a college in the United States of America.

I completed midwifery school while I was working on leaving Nigeria for America. I had no idea whether it was going to be hard or easy; I was going to give it all I could in order to get what I wanted. Then I needed to work with the Student Advisory Committee (SAC). This was a body set up to screen prospective students to make sure the candidate met all the requirements before they could be sent to the American Embassy to apply for a student visa. The Student Advisory Committee also checked to make sure that the prospective student had been admitted to an approved college abroad. The first school I was admitted to was a community college, but the Student Advisory Committee disapproved of that.

Instead, they gave me a list of approved schools in the U.S. Finally, I was admitted into an "approved school"- it was Anna Maria College in Paxton, Massachusetts. I was thrilled, and I was so happy. Yes!

Then there was a roadblock. With the admission letter came a "Guarantor's Form" that needed to be signed. The person to sign this form must have 6,000 naira approximately in their bank account. That was about $12,000 American dollars back then. This person must attach their bank statement to the signed guarantor's form. I had nobody close to me; neither did I know anyone who had that kind of money. What was I going to do? Would this end my dreams? By this time, I was still working in the OR at Ramat Specialist Hospital. I asked all the surgeons, one by one, if any of them could sign the guarantor's form for me. Whomever I talked to, looked at me as if I was crazy. They said, "Who has that kind of money tucked away? I do not think you will find anybody to help you with this. That is too much money to be expected from an individual." I had thought that those surgeons were loaded with money; I never thought I was going to have any problem with them doing this for me. I did not need any money from them; I just needed the form signed and their bank statement attached. I found that it was impossible to get this done within the hospital, so I started looking for help outside of the hospital. Still, I could not find anybody to commit to this request whether they had the stated amount or not.

I had done all I could without success, I then turned to the Lord for His divine intervention. This time I prayed, not my will, but Thine be done, Lord, at your own timing. It was hard to believe and to accept that this was the end of my dream to go to America. Well, if that's it, let me move back home and get a job at a nearby hospital. I thought this would enable me to be close to my aging parents, taking care of them and maybe settling down.

In my desperation, it then came to mind a family that had my last name and they had a big transportation business. I went to them with the hope that they may be able to help me by signing the guarantor's form for me. When I went there, I met the manager who may have noticed how desperate I was. I sat down in his office and told him why I came to him. He asked me to go on a date with him. He told me that if I went out on a date with him, he would sign the form for me. Frustrated and shocked at this unexpected request, I said to him, "Is that the only condition that you would sign this form for me?" "Yes," he answered. "Thank you very much and goodbye" I said to him, getting up to leave. I walked out of his office with tears filling up my eyes and I tried to control it until I got out of the building. Being so overwhelmed, I made my way outside and I lost it. Crying so hard, I did not even realize that it was raining heavily. I walked right into the rain with my handbag in my hand and an un-opened umbrella. I cried so hysterically that my tears and the rain drenched me. Thank God, it was raining because that concealed my tears and frustration from other passersby. Who would have imagined a young woman soaked in the rain with an un-opened umbrella in her hand! I cried so much that when the rain finally stopped, the tears were still running down my cheeks. I then stood by the roadside waiting for any form of public transportation to take me back to the hospital. I was not a worrying type; I would always act or do something instead of worrying about what I could not do anything about. For the first time, I was so upset and disappointed that I could not sleep that night. I could not think of anything else to do. About 4:00 AM that morning, I got up to pray. In my prayer, I acknowledged God; I also told Him that I had exhausted all my options. "Now I am leaving it up to you, Lord. How and when you will do it for me is unknown to me. My hope is in you Lord." I prayed, believing that God would open doors for me at His own timing and resources. After this earnest prayer, I felt peace within me and then I fell asleep. I woke up the following day about 10:00AM, feeling happy, as if I had not even a thing to worry about. This meant so much to me. I was never a worrywart. The following day, I went to work uneventfully.

CHAPTER 12

Relocation

Since I thought that I may or may not go to America, (and even if I did go, I did not know when) I decided to hand in a transfer letter to the current hospital I was working in and move back home near my parents. I did that the following week. Then I went to the Ministry of Health headquarters in Calabar, in my state of origin. They would arrange for a job in any nearby hospital with a vacancy for a registered Nurse/Midwife. I was offered a job at St. Margaret Hospital in Calabar right away. It was the biggest hospital in my state. I had lived in this city with my brother and his wife after high school. By now, my brother had been transferred to Oron in the same state, so he was not nearby. I turned down the job offer because of the distance from my parents- about 4 hours. I told the Human Resource woman who interviewed me that it was too far and I also told her that I did not know anybody in Calabar. "I have never lived alone outside the school premises and I wouldn't even know where to start from in this big city." She said to me, "You are now a grown up woman. You have to start learning how to live on your own outside of the school and hospital confinements. It seems you have led a protected life all along." "Yes, that is true," I replied, "I was always either at a boarding school, at home with my parents or at my brother's house. I have never been on my own; I do not even know how to start out." She said, "Well, this is your chance to try it and learn how. You have to start somewhere and some day. You will not be with your parents or in a boarding school forever. For this reason, I will not change your job in Calabar. Go and give it a trial. First, find yourself an apartment to rent and then get yourself settled and go from there. I am giving you three months to try. If you cannot make it, then come back to me and I will change it. I just want you to try it first. It may not be as difficult as you think." "Okay," I said, "Thank you very much." My heart was beating very fast as I walked out of the Human Resource woman's office. I could not have imagined living alone in the city---WOW!

Walking out of the Human Resource woman's office in the Ministry of Health in Calabar, I stood across the street to catch a taxi to take me home to my parents. Standing out there all by myself, I was trying to imagine my apartment-to-be and anxious at the thought of living alone for the first time. I was so carried away in my thoughts that a couple of taxis had gone by without my notice. I was brought back to reality by a voice calling me by my unofficial name, a name only used by people close to me at home. I turned and a private car had stopped nearby, so I stepped forward to check out who this person was. I realized that this was a distant relative of my mother who was also my teacher in my second high school where I attended after the Nigerian Civil War. I had met her in that high school for the first time. Back then, she told me how she was related to my mother, and my mom had confirmed it. She had been very kind to me when I had arrived in my new high school. Once high school was over for me, I had never had any contact with her, so I was thrilled to see her now. She told me to get into her car, which I did excitedly, and she took me to her house that was close by. Once we got to her house and out of the car, we hugged each other for a long time and I kept saying, "Could this be true? This is unbelievable." I was so happy to see her that all my problems seemed to have disappeared. She had a gorgeous mansion in the housing estate in Calabar. When we had first met, she was a young unmarried woman at the high school where she taught. At this time in her life, she was married with three children ages seven, five and three years old. To me she was very successful and rich. Her husband was not home yet, and her two older children were still in school. She had a maid that cared for the children and did house chores. She asked the maid to fix something for us to eat while we sat trying to catch up after eight years of separation from each other. I let her go first, and she told me as much as she could. A lot of good and a few bad encounters on her life's journey. One of the things she told me was that she had been planning to leave for America in her past. It was not working out and she was still here today in Nigeria. She said she was okay now, but she still felt disappointed for not leaving for America as she had wished. I tried to console her by saying, "Well, you settled down, you have these beautiful children, a loving husband and all this wealth." She answered me and said, "Going to America could have given me a lot more than this."

I let her finish her stories before I started mine. I told her about my current educational achievements and my future aspirations. It was not funny at all when I told her where I was now stuck in my preparation to leave for America. We both looked at each other—there was the similarity between us. I told her there was nothing more I could do, so I have left it in God's hands and I am waiting to see what happens next. I told her for that reason, I had decided to move back home to take care of my parents but instead I was currently given a position at St. Margaret hospital here in Calabar to start working the following week, on a male medical unit. She was very happy for me to work at St. Margaret Hospital. Then she turned around and said to me, "My husband can sign the guarantor's form for you and give you the bank statement too. Talk to him about it." I looked at her with mixed feelings. I had never met her husband before. Not knowing him made it feel impossible to even "Go there." I also told her that I needed to get an apartment to stay in, expressing my fear of living alone for the first time. I told her what had transpired in the Ministry of Health, how the Human Resource's woman told me to give it a trial period now and if it did not work out, only then would she assign me somewhere else. After telling my relative all I could, she asked me to go to my parents' home, get my belongings and come to stay with her until her husband could find an apartment for me. "What a miracle" I thought. I was so happy and thankful to her. Within me, I was praising the Lord for answered prayers. At least for the moment, I had someone I knew in town. We had a big lunch at her house; she gave me a hug and said, "See you on Sunday."

I went back home and spent that whole week with my parents. It was very enjoyable and I was so happy. I told my mother that I had transferred from where I was working at Umuahia in Imo state to a hospital in Calabar in preparation for leaving to America for further studies, even though I did not know the exact time this would materialize. Mom was happy about this and she advised me not to tell other people about it for safety reasons. I told her about my encounter with this relative of hers, my former high school teacher, how she had asked me to come and stay with her until her husband found an apartment for me and that I would be leaving for her house on Sunday evening. Mom was very pleased with that. She started packing boxes with cooking pots, pans, utensils and whatever she imagined I would need to start out.

Finally, Sunday evening came and I left my parents' home to start out in the real world, on my own with a suitcase and boxes of stuff my mother gave me. I did not really know all the contents of the boxes my mom had packed for me, it did not matter, since I would be able to work at the hospital and would hopefully afford whatever I would need. I arrived at my relative's house as expected. She was home and waiting for me. Her maid helped me with my suitcase and the boxes I had.

My relative showed me the room she had prepared for me. I was very grateful to her for being so kind and accommodating. I trusted her and felt comfortable with her. The children looked at me as a stranger, which I was then to them. "This is your Auntie," their mother introduced me to them. The first day I had gone there before, was a weekday. The two older children had been in school and her husband was not home, but on this Sunday, I was able to meet the whole family. Her husband was a quiet, peaceful man, who welcomed me into his home and told me to feel free and if I had any concerns to let his wife know. I thanked him, while still trying to figure him out and my entire new environment.

I started work at St. Margaret Hospital the following day on a male medical unit using public transportation, since I did not have a car. I had orientation for one week, and then I was set on my own, as an RN with resources and staff I could fall back on if I needed help. Once I was through with the orientation, I started working the rotating shift. It was a forty-hour workweek of 7:00 AM-3:00 PM for one week, followed by 1:00 -9:00 PM the following week with two days off for each week worked; finally, we rotated to nights, 9:00 PM-7:00 AM for seven straight days and then had nine days off. When we came back from the nine days off, we were started back on days and the cycle continued. We could not choose which shift we wanted to work since all the nurses and the nurse's aides needed to do all the rotations. We were only exempted from rotating shifts if we were in a management position in the hospital where we worked days, or 8:00 AM-4:00 PM,

Monday through Friday, no weekends or holidays. This was quite enticing for me to decide to go back to school. "I did not want to work nights all my life, especially if I was married, but it was okay for me then," I thought.

I continued working at St. Margaret's Hospital for four months, still living with my relation and her family. By the second month, I asked her if her husband was still looking for an apartment for me, since I had not heard anything about it. Her answer was "No he is not. Please stay here, there is no need looking for an apartment. This house is big enough. I do not want you to go anywhere else." Hmmm, I did not expect this. My intention was not to be here permanently, so I said to her, "Please tell him to keep looking, I only planned to be here temporarily." She replied, "Do not worry about it, as far as I am concerned you are not going anywhere. For your information, I am taking a vacation next week and I am travelling out. I count it a blessing that I have a trustworthy person to leave my children with to take a vacation." I stood there speechless, looking at her like, "excuse me, what do you mean?" True enough, the following week, she was gone for two weeks. I took care of the whole family until she returned. By the grace of the Lord, all went well in her absence.

I did not talk to my relative's husband about my problem with the guarantor's form as she had asked me earlier to do. When she had told me that her husband could help me with the guarantor's form, I had then asked my relative to talk to him about it for me, but she had said no, I should talk to him myself. I did not feel comfortable talking to her husband since they had gone out of their way to accommodate me. I felt that was enough.

In early December that year, 1978, my relative became sick and was hospitalized for a week at St. Margaret's Hospital on our female medical unit. Between my taking care of her family, going to work and then visiting her in the hospital, I had my hands full. I was determined to give it my best. It was at this point that my relative's husband asked his own driver to transport me to work and wherever I wanted to go. This was a great help. With readily available transportation, I was able to juggle all my responsibilities much more easily.

One evening, I was riding with my relative's husband to visit his wife in the hospital and he said to me, "Thank you so much for all your help. So many people from my wife's side of the family have lived with us and I cannot compare any of them to you. You have been so helpful. I do not know how to express my gratitude to you. My wife talked to me about your problem regarding your Guarantor's Form for furthering your education. I will sign it for you and give you a bank statement. I can do all that for you. I thought you would ask me, but it seems you would never have asked. That is why I brought it up." I thanked him for his compliments and their flexibility in taking me into their home for these four months. I told him that if he could help me with my educational and financial problems, that would be awesome. When we arrived at the hospital, we were told that his wife was getting better and that she was to be discharged home the following day, though she was still weak. We were told to "push fluids" with her when she gets home, since she was still dehydrated.

Either the earlier conversation my relative's husband had with me on our way to the hospital was pushed aside, because I felt like it was too good to be true or I was too busy to let it sink in until three days after his wife was home from the hospital. She was getting better and stronger, and somewhat gradually resuming her role at home. It was a great relief for me that she was getting better. Yes, now I could think. "What did her husband tell me on our way to the hospital? I think he said he could help me, for real. Please dear Lord let this be what he said, if I am not mistaken or losing my mind." The following week, my relative's husband asked me for the guarantor's form which I gave to him. The following day he returned it to me signed, with his bank statement attached. He also said, to expedite things for me, he was taking me to the Student Advisory Committee (SAC) himself. By the third day, everything was all set; the appointment date for me to go to the American Embassy for a student visa was scheduled for me by the Student Advisory Committee. The SAC gave me a sealed letter to take with me to the American Embassy in Lagos, the capital of Nigeria then. This letter contained all the necessary information to confirm that I had met the requirements to obtain a student visa to go to the United States of America.

I went home to my village for Christmas and told my parents all that had happened and made them aware that I may not visit them again before I leave for America. Everything happened very quickly, within two weeks, which was a lot sooner than I had anticipated. It is good though, I said. "The Lord has answered my prayers, to Him be the glory."

My mother was the only one that I told the date I was going to Lagos, for the student visa and she promised to uphold me in a special prayer that day. We had a great Christmas holiday. I had not spent Christmas at home with my parents for about five years, so this was very, very special for me. The thought of leaving for America meant I might never spend another Christmas with my parents, so I made the best of this one. My parents enjoyed me and I had a blast with them. My sisters and their children came home to my parents' house. We had a phenomenal time together. I had a memorable Christmas that year, but I was thinking still, that this might be the last Christmas I would spend with my parents.

My immediate older sister, Alice had promised to give me a set amount of money to help me if I ever succeeded in leaving for the United States of America. As things progressed rather quickly, I had hinted to her that when I came home for Christmas I would collect the money from her. When I stopped at her house for the money, she said to me, "I need you to come with me to Uyo to see a friend of mine." This was a two-hour ride to her friend who, by the time we got there, was at work. My sister was acting sad and non-verbal on our way there. Once we stepped out of the public transportation, I noticed tears in her eyes. "What is the matter?" I asked her. At this point, she would not talk and she was overwhelmed. I still did not understand why she was crying. We arrived at the hospital where we met Nkoyo, my sister Alice's friend. She came outside to meet us. The moment my sister set her eyes on her, she cried so uncontrollably that she could not talk. Nkoyo gave her a hug, turned to me and asked, "What happened, did somebody die?" I said to her, "I do not really understand. I came to get the money my sister promised to give me for my travels and she brought me here, but is now crying so uncontrollably." Nkoyo asked me, "What was the amount of the money and for what purpose?" I gave her the answer to her question. She then went back to her Hospital unit, came back with a personal check for the exact amount of money, and gave it to my sister. I thanked her and my sister tearfully thanked her too, then we went to the bank and cashed the check. My sister gave me the money and I left to go back home to my parents. I found out later that Alice's husband had borrowed the money from her and had not yet paid her back. My sister Alice went to borrow that money for me and ended up paying it back to her friend, Nkoyo. What a phenomenal sister and friend they were! I went back to Calabar, to my relative's house where I had been living to get ready to go to Lagos to get my student visa.

My appointment with the American Embassy for my Visa was scheduled for January 2, 1979. I told my nurse manager about it, requesting three days off, one each for travelling by airplane, back and forth and one day at the American Embassy. She was happy for me and suggested a week off. I told her that I thought that was too many days, but she said she wanted me to be on the safe side. She finally said, "Take four days; you are cutting it too lean by requesting for only three days." I accepted the four days and thanked her for being so reasonable and I left.

This would be the first time I had ever travelled by plane. My relative and her husband brought me to the Calabar airport. I bought my flight ticket and I only had one carry-on for luggage. They stayed with me until I was checked in. It was about a forty-five minute plane ride from Calabar to Lagos. I then took a taxi from the local airport in Lagos to my brother-in-law's (my oldest sister's husband) house who was living in Lagos at the time, where I spent the rest of the day. Early the following morning my brother- in-law asked his driver to take me to the American Embassy. When we got there at 4:00 AM, people were already lined up outside waiting for the office to be opened at 8:00 AM. I was number 15. My brother in-law knew the protocol and had advised me to arrive very early. We waited in line until the opening of the American Embassy and the line grew very long. Once we were inside, there were four lines formed in front of the windows where we were attended. The letter that I was given from the Student Advisory Committee was taken from me, and I was asked a couple of questions and my passport was stamped. I had no problem, everything went well, and I was back to Calabar by the third day around 10:00AM. I went back to work for one week. I told my Nurse Manager that everything went well and I was leaving the country for America the following week. She was happy for me and she removed me from the hospital work schedule.

On my last day at St. Margaret Hospital, I said my quiet goodbyes to a few close friends at the end of my shift, telling them that I was leaving, without telling them where I was going. My leaving was unexpected since I was new to this hospital. I also told one of my patients who had spent two weeks on the unit, a very nice elderly man. I told him I was no longer going to work for the hospital, this was my last day, and I wanted to say goodbye to him. I wished him a quick recovery. This patient had always addressed me as "Ama-Asi," he never called me "Nurse." He said to me, "Ama-Asi," which is an endearing name for a young woman, "Why are you abandoning me here? Who is going to take care of me when you are gone?" "Oh!" I said, "There are many nurses here who will care for you." He said, "Not like you. You took great care of me; I will miss you a lot. I wish you well wherever you are going. I wish I could stop you from leaving, but it seems like everything is all set for you to go." "Goodbye," I said to him, "I pray you feel better soon."

CHAPTER 13

My Last Days in Nigeria Before Leaving for America

Now that I was done with work, I had one week to complete all my preparations to leave for the United States of America. My flight was booked with PANAM airline; I received my flight ticket and the itinerary. I bought whatever I thought I would need and had a suitcase packed plus one carry-on for luggage. I bought one sweater to take with me, since I did not know what the weather would be like in the North East of the U.S in January.

I had gone to the bank to send my tuition to the school in the U.S. The woman that handled the foreign exchange transaction that day was not being very nice to me. In my previous dealings with her, she had remarked that many young girls had been bothering her with transactions for leaving the country and she thought that they could not afford it. I was new in town and I had not yet transferred my money from the previous place where I worked to this bank. As I was putting everything together, I had enough money in my account and a little bit of extra finances at the end of my transaction. I do not think she was happy that I could afford to leave. I went in to her office, she asked me to sit down and I did. I gave her all the information she needed for the transaction and she told me what I was going to pay. "You can take that money out of my account," I said. When she pulled up my account and saw the amount and that I had enough money, she got up without saying anything to me and left the building. I sat there waiting for her for a very long time. I had no choice due to the time constraint. I waited patiently for over an hour and she never came back. The two young men who were working near that area whispered to each other saying, "Oh, Mama has walked out on that young woman and she is going to be gone for a very long time." I heard what they said, but since they were not talking to me, I sat there quietly. I could not leave the bank because of my limited time; I had to get this taken care of today, come what may.

Finally, one of the two young men came over to help me. He did everything that needed to be done for half the price the woman who had left was going to charge me. I was very grateful to him. I thanked him and told him that I was leaving in a few days. He told me that his dad was a patient at St. Margaret hospital, in the male medical unit on bed 1. This was my patient and the only patient I had told that I was leaving the hospital, the one who used to call me Ama-Asi. I told him that his dad was such a nice man, even when he was sick. I said, "I hope your dad feels better soon, goodbye."

He handed me a folded piece of paper that I did not open until I was outside the bank. The other young man said to me, "Remember us when you get there, we too would like to come to America." I said okay to him and goodbye. As I walked out of the bank, I opened the folded paper the other young man gave me, which I still had in my hand. It had his full name and address. "Hmm, I thought, what does he want me to do with this? I will be leaving in a few days." It did not make any sense to me, so I tore the paper and threw it away within the bank premises. His name and address was of no use to me, period. I was leaving the country.

I was able to visit my parents for one last time to bid them goodbye before leaving. My mom gave me a lot of money that I did not expect. I was worried that she did not have enough money for herself, so I was going to give her whatever amount that was left. She refused to take any money from me, saying, "Take all the amount you have and whatever I gave you, you will need all of it. You are going so far away from home and there is no one there to help you if you need it. You are going to be on your own." My mother blessed me and told me that she would uphold me in her prayers. "By the way," she said, "I am concerned about your finding a husband in America, since you are going so far away from home." "Mom," I said, "When the Lord opens doors, He provides for ALL my needs, including a husband. Do not worry about such things. All will be well with me by His Grace." We talked about all we could, knowing I would be gone for a long time. It was then that it hit me, the probability of losing either or both of my parents while I would be so far away. With that thought occurring to me, the moment changed. I became emotional and tried to touch on pertinent issues in case I never saw either of my parents alive again. As we were talking, my mom touched on my thought of their destiny - death. She told me and I knew it to be true, that she had worked extremely hard all her married life to raise us to the best of her ability and none of us had disappointed her whatever path we had decided to take in our lives. She said she was very proud of all her children and was contented with how her life had turned out; up to this moment we were sharing together. As she continued talking, she expressed the thought that if I were to settle down and be done with college, get married and have children, she would feel complete, her joy would be full, and she would feel her mission had been accomplished on earth. Then when death came, she would go very peacefully. In my response to what she just said, I told her that the good Lord would grant her heart's desire and may even bless her more than she expected. Then she said, "When you go, do not stay in America for too long. I do not have any control over when the Lord calls me home, (meaning death). I hope this is not an eternal goodbye." Now we both realized what could happen and we were both in tears. I hugged my mom as if I never wanted to let go of her, crying very hard. I did not like the idea of us parting in this way and I started apologizing to her for my being so emotional. She accepted my apology and told me not to worry about it because parting was hard enough. Moreover, not knowing if she would see me again before the Lord calls her made it even harder. "I will try to hang in there till we meet again," she said. It was one of the hardest goodbyes I ever had to say.

Coming back from my parents' home to my relative's house in Calabar was not easy. I had mixed feelings of both joy for my success, and sadness, for leaving all my loved ones, especially my parents, behind. I was in a kind of mood I could not describe. This was real. I was leaving home for good, I had to deal with it by keeping a low profile, and I kept to myself a lot. My relative's children tried to cheer me up, but knowing how much I was going to miss them did not help me. My relative had cautioned me to be careful as my departure day drew nearer. She did not want any mishap or accident, all she wanted for me was a smooth departure.

Finally, my departure day for the United States of America came on January 13, 1979. My relative and her husband saw me off at the local airport in Calabar. Not one single person in my immediate family was there to see me off. I missed them already and none of them was here? That hurt! My brother lived an hour away from me, the rest of my siblings lived about three hours away; they all could have come to see me off. That saddened me a lot. I held back my tears and instead showed my gratitude to this wonderful family. They stayed with me until it was time for me to board the plane at 8:45 AM. Once I mustered the courage to say goodbye to them with a smile, I went on the plane and I lost it. The tears came running down my cheeks, so uncontrollably that the young man who sat next to me in the plane tried to console me but he could not. He thought I had lost a loved one and that is why I was crying so much. I could not even talk. He pulled me to himself, gave me a big hug and said, "Whatever you are going through, I pray the Lord to give you the strength to bear it." I said thank you to him in between sobs. He left me alone and did not try to talk to me anymore.

I arrived in Lagos about 10:00 AM at the local airport and I took a taxi to my brother-in-law's house to spend the rest of the day. On my arrival at my in-law's house, I was surprised to see my nephew again, who had been living in America. He said he was back in Nigeria on vacation for two weeks. It was so good to see him. However, for my personality, and not having any idea of what to expect in America, I did not think to ask my nephew any questions about the United States. My guiding principle had always been "When the Lord opens the door for me; He guides, provides and protects me." For this reason, I did not get scared or worried over what I could not do anything about. I leaned on the Lord to see me through and He has never failed me. I thought I just have to "Trust in God."

The PANAM international flight was scheduled to depart the Murtala Muhammed International Airport in Lagos, Nigeria at 10:00 PM for New York. It was a direct flight. I was supposed to be at the airport at least by 6:00 PM. In the company of my nephew, his father (my brother-in-law) and the driver, I was taken to the airport. In a conversation on our way, my nephew asked me what I had handy for warm clothes. "I have this sweater if I need it." He then said, "Is that all you have?" "Yes, that should be enough I guess," was my reply. My nephew did not say anything more. When we got to the airport, he gave me a kind of jacket that I did not know what it was used for; it was too heavy to be a raincoat, so I asked him why he gave it to me and for what purpose. He said to me, "It is very cold over there at this time of the year in January, you will need this jacket. It may not even be enough for you." I could not imagine that any part of the world could be so cold. My country, Nigeria, is warm all year round; you rarely even need a sweater. Oh well, I took the heavy jacket from him, not believing that I would need it. My brother-in-law and nephew stayed with me until I was checked in. I thanked them and we said our goodbyes. "See you soon," I said to my nephew as we parted. I then waited in an area designated for the PANAM flight departure until boarding time. This was my first time ever in an international airport.

CHAPTER 14

Going to the United States of America

Our airplane left Lagos at 10:00 PM. I was lucky to have a seat next to the window and once I was seated, I did not get up. It happened that the weather was so bad in New York City that we could not land there. It was announced that the plane was being diverted to Bermuda and we would be there until the weather cleared in New York City enough for us to land safely. It was here that I got up for the first time and walked around, and actually went outside for a short period to stretch my legs. Some people went further away from the plane. Not me. The fear of the unknown prevented me from taking anything for granted. I had prayed for a safe trip so I had to be careful and vigilant. When it was time for us to depart Bermuda, the announcement was made and every passenger got in and we left for New York City.

I then had a connecting flight from New York to Boston. When I arrived in Boston, I went through security. I did not understand what was happening. I just stood in the line with the others, who came out of the same plane. I was checked and allowed to pass through. In observing what was going on, I noted that some people were checked and allowed to pass; some were checked and detained for whatever reason. I felt bad for the people that were detained, prayed and hoped they would be okay. Once I was done with immigration, I had to head to baggage claim to get my suitcase. I did not step outside when I switched planes in New York, so I had no clue what the weather would be outside in Boston, Massachusetts in January.

I claimed my suitcase and stepped outside to look for a ride to Worcester, Mass. The cold air hit my face so hard that my eyes and nose started running instantly. It was so cold, I was shocked people could live and survive in a place that cold. Immediately, I went right back into the building, threw on my sweater and the winter jacket my nephew had given me. Now I know what it was for. I was shivering in spite of the warm clothing. It was scary to step outside again, but I had no choice since I had to get to Worcester. While inside the airport again, I asked an airport worker how and where I could get a means of transportation to Worcester, since I did not want to stay outside to ask. I was told where to wait for a big bus and what time the bus would be there. This was very useful information for me. I stepped out about five minutes before the expected time for the bus to arrive. It was so cold that I thought I was going to die. The jacket was helpful, but I had a dress on, my hands and feet seemed to be frozen and I could not feel anything. As I stood there shivering, an elderly woman noticed how cold I was and said to me, "Poor kid, did you just arrive? Where are you from?" "Yes, I just arrived from Nigeria and I am waiting to catch a bus to Worcester." Not knowing the right pronunciation of Worcester, the woman could not make out where I said I was going. I wrote it down on a piece of paper for her to read, "Oh, Wooster," she said, from there I learned and kept practicing the correct way Worcester was pronounced. She said I was standing at the right place and the bus would roll in shortly. I thanked her for her help as she walked away. True enough, a big bus rolled in and many people got on. As I was boarding, I asked the bus driver to drop me off in Worcester. I thought he would be dropping people off as he passed through all the towns and cities before we got to Worcester, since that was how it was where I came from. He looked at me quizzically without saying anything. It turned out to be a nonstop ride from the Logan airport in Boston to downtown Worcester.

I arrived in Worcester, Massachusetts on January 14, 1979 at 7:00 PM on Main Street. Everyone got off the bus, I stepped out and it was dark and extremely cold. Other people that got off the bus knew where they were going. Before I knew it, everybody was gone and the bus left. I did not know where to go or what to do. Personal cars were passing; nobody was walking by. I felt as if I were in a different world. It was scary. What should I do? Luckily, I saw a taxi coming. I was relieved, thinking that I would get a ride. I stepped out and waved for the taxi driver to stop to give me a ride but he did not stop. A couple more taxis passed by and I kept waving but none of them stopped. I crossed over to the other side of the street thinking that I probably stood on the wrong side of the street and that's why they did not stop for me. The same thing happened. Not knowing what else to do, I prayed, "Dear Lord thank you for bringing me safely from Nigeria to Worcester. You've been with me this far. Please Lord send your guardian angel to lead me to Cohasset Street. I do not know what else to do than to trust in you and that's what I am doing now. Amen." After that prayer, I had this wonderful peace and calmness within me.

I decided not to wave at any taxis that passed by. I stood there looking around, waiting for a miracle. As I waited, I saw a woman coming out of one of the buildings. I ran to her saying, "Excuse me please." The woman stopped until I got to her. I explained my situation to her and she said, "Yeah, it's too cold, the cab will not stop. You have to call them." "How do I call them?" I asked the woman. This was the era of pay telephones on the streets. She said to me, "I will call one for you, what's your name?" I told her my name, she made the call and told me to stay right there, and a cab will show up for me. I was so grateful and thankful to her. I learned from this experience that taxi drivers do not stop to pick up passengers in this city. You have to call them on the phone first. No sooner did she leave, and then my taxi stopped by to give me a ride to Cohasset Street. I got into the taxi and thanked the Lord for answering my prayers. Not having any clue where I was in pitch darkness, I prayed for the taxi driver to take me to the right address. He could have taken me anywhere and I would not have known the difference. I sat in the back of the taxi, observing all the street names we passed, hoping that Cohasset Street would show up soon. Finally, it did, I was so relieved. The taxi driver dropped me off; I paid him and thanked him.

I rang the doorbell to the apartment number as my nephew had instructed me, for his landlady to let me into the building. When she responded through an intercom, by asking, "Who is it?" I was startled and surprised since I had never used a doorbell or an intercom before. I told her who I was and then she opened the main door to the building for me from her apartment. She also told me to come up to the third floor, where she met me and then opened the door to my nephew's apartment for me. I had arrived at my final destination at last! I walked into the living room, putting my luggage down; I knelt down to thank God for bringing me safely all the way to America. It still seemed like a dream even though it was real.

Here I was with no idea of what to expect. I walked around to check the apartment out. There were two bedrooms, a living room, a kitchen and a bathroom with some closets. I figured out that the bigger bedroom was my nephew's, so I put my things in the smaller one. I then undressed, took a shower and went to the kitchen to find something to eat. Luckily for me, I found some leftover food in the refrigerator, which I warmed up and ate before I went to bed at 9:30 PM. About 11:20 PM or so that same Saturday evening, I was wakened by some people coming into the apartment. It was my nephew's girlfriend and her friend. They were surprised to find me in the apartment sleeping, but said they were very happy for my safe arrival. They apologized for waking me up, and then left me alone. I went back to sleep, since I was so tired from my journey and finally woke up around 10:00 AM Sunday morning to an empty house. I thought there were two women who came in here last night or was it a dream? In addition to the new and strange environment, looking outside through the windows, it was snowing. Everything outside was covered with snow, a white fluffy stuff that gave an air of purity and beauty. Everywhere looked so clean but it was still extremely cold. Many people were in cars driving by. Only very few people were walking outside if any at all. It seemed to be too cold for people to walk around outside. The two women returned at 2:00 PM in the afternoon. They said they had gone to church.

Since I had arrived on a Saturday evening, I rested and unpacked on Sunday. My nephew's girlfriend told me that she would take me out on Monday to show me around, do some shopping for my necessities and stop at my college for registration. It was her day off, so she wanted to help me get situated. This was very generous and thoughtful of her. She had a car, which made moving around easier. Monday morning, she took me to my new college, which was Anna Maria in Paxton. I registered and bought my books at the bookstore. At registration, I was given a course catalog, a syllabus and my class schedule. I then had a tour of the campus, to make sure I knew where I was supposed to be when my classes started. Once we were done with the tour of my college, my nephew's girlfriend took me shopping mostly for winter clothing and boots, which I now needed for the snow. She showed me where I would take the city bus to downtown Worcester and where my college bus was scheduled to pick us up to go to campus for classes. I learned the times the campus bus was leaving the City Hall. Finally, we went grocery shopping. From there she drove me around trying to show me as much as she could of the City of Worcester. Everything was so new and strange. I could not grasp as much as I would have liked to. I appreciated her so much. If my nephew's girlfriend was not around, I do not know what I would have done. Since she had access to my class schedule, she started looking for a job for me, something that would fit with my college schedule. She found me a job as a home health aide for an elderly woman, which was two days a week for four hours. This would be just enough for me to start out with. I was excited!

CHAPTER 15

Life in the United States of America

After many years of struggling and wondering when it was going to happen, it only took two weeks after my relative's husband signed the guarantor's form, before I was on my way to America! The timing of this could not have been better because my college classes started at Anna Maria College right away in mid-January and I had classes Monday-Friday, from 8:00 AM-2:30 PM. I first worked my part time job for a month and then my nephew's girlfriend helped me find a full time job in a nursing home as a nurse's aide. I worked full time nights with every other weekend off to survive financially. At that time, I did not know any better to have asked for a more suitable schedule at work. I just took what I was offered without any negotiation. I could have opted to work a twelve-hour shift every Friday, Saturday and Sunday, which was considered full time and then have the rest of the week free for my classes. Instead, I worked nights, leaving work in the morning to go straight to the college. It was not easy but God's grace and my determination to succeed carried me through successfully. I was sleepy in some of my classes because I had worked all night before coming to class. I never told anyone about it. My mindset was to do well in school, and pass all my exams, which I accomplished. In my country then, I would not have had to work while attending a university for nursing. I could have been sponsored by the government. The only problem I had with that was I would not have been allowed to attend at will since the government controlled the entrance rate, so I would have had to wait until there was space for me. I felt I did not have the time to wait. This was one of the reasons I decided to look for admission into a university outside my country. This cost me a lot of money, but I was able to do what I wanted to do in my own timing. It was somewhat new to me to be in school and work at the same time.

I had many adjustments to make about life in America. Now, since I lived in New England and it seemed many things were done differently. People minded their business. You did not talk to people you did not know. You were lonely in the midst of many people. A couple of times when I greeted people, they looked surprised, some responded and some just ignored me. It did not bother me whether people responded to me or not. I came from a small village and community where we always greeted people we just met. I recall an occasion that I joined a woman at the bus stop on Chandler street, close by the then City Hospital in Worcester. I said good morning to her. She turned, looking strangely at me and moved away. Therefore, I said to her, "How are you today?" She was taken aback and finally said, "I am so sorry, I am in my own world. I am really worried about my daughter who is on admission at that hospital," pointing to City Hospital. She is very sick and I am worried about her." I empathized with her. Then she started talking to me. By the time the bus came, she acted like we knew each other before or like we were old friends. She told me her name and where she lived, I only told her my name. She got off the bus before me and we bid each other goodbye. I never saw her again. What I learned from this is sometimes people are lost in their own thoughts. They don't mean to be rude. By reaching out to her, she was able to tell me what was bothering her and both of us felt better for each other. Well, since I came from a small village where we knew everyone or at school, it never occurred to me to be cautious of people I did not know. I still say hello to people I do not know a lot more than other people do.

At work, I had to adjust a lot to how things were done. We never had nursing homes for the elderly in Nigeria then. We took care of our elderly ones within the family unit. Once I started working, I was very upset thinking that some people abandoned their elderly parents by putting them in a nursing home instead of caring for them at home. I felt then that if our parents cared for us when we were helpless and dependent as children, then it would be our responsibility to care for them when they were old and helpless. It was like role reversal yet, instead of taking care of their elderly parents, the children sent them to nursing homes to be cared for by total strangers. I felt then that this practice was very unfair to the older people. For this reason, I was very empathic to my patients. I cared for them as if they were my parents. I did not understand then that people sometimes feel their relatives would be better off in a nursing home with fulltime caregivers who are knowledgeable about their health care. I had many culture shocks and I had to learn very quickly to adjust to my new world.

I had my routine down pat, working 40 hours a week, 11:00 PM to 7:00 AM with every other weekend off. I went from work straight to the college bus stop to get to my class, since I did not have any time to reach home. My classes started at 8:00 AM and ended at 2:30 PM, Monday through Friday. I had to rush from work to catch the school bus at city hall by 7:30 AM.

Since I started in the spring semester, some of my courses' sequence were not in order. For example, I started with Anatomy and Physiology Part 2 and had to go back to take Part 1 in the fall. For me, it did not make any difference. I took some of the courses that I needed at other nearby colleges and transferred them to my college. I felt that I needed to be done with the bachelor's program as soon as possible, so that I could go back home to Nigeria to see my parents. I did not want to delay and end up losing either of them. I felt I needed one more chance to see them to deal with the fact that I could lose them without seeing either of them again since I was so far away from them.

I had sent a full year's tuition and the boarding fees from the bank in Nigeria to the college before I left Nigeria. With that in mind, I thought I would be all set financially when I got to America. I did not anticipate any problem once the money was sent on time. I was then informed by the college that the money never came. I did not know what was going on. School had started and they were asking me about my tuition. I gave the college the name and the address of the bank I had remitted the money through to contact them as to why the money was not here. I also contacted the bank and they said they did not know what happened to the money. Well, I could not let anything stand in the way of my education and success, whatever it was going to take. I would make it by the grace of God. This made me work harder to support myself in the U.S in case the money never came. In the summer of that year, 1979, I took some courses in other colleges that offered them, part time. This gave me the opportunity to work more hours and obtain a part time job in addition to the full time job I already had. With all that, I was able to save enough for my tuition and even had extra.

During that summer, I went to driving school and got my first driving license without owning a car. My nephew's girlfriend teased me about "having a driver's license without a car to drive." I responded to her by saying that was perfectly all right with me. I knew myself; I have never compared myself to others or had to conform to other people's norms. I know I am unique and I have and will always accept, appreciate and love myself for who I am. Whatever other people are doing or saying is none of my business. This attitude makes it difficult for people to offend me. So my nephew's girlfriend then said to me, "Oh! Excuse me!" "You are very excused," I responded and she left me alone. She wanted to rub it in because she had a car and I did not. If only she knew how contented and happy I was for all I had accomplished up to that point. She also had no idea what my destiny was going to be. My nephew's girlfriend completed her education that year, earning a Master's Degree in Education, I think. She went back to Nigeria for 2 years.

In early November of that year, 1979, the long expected money came from Nigeria. It was then that I learned there had been an issue with the tax clearance in the Central Bank of Nigeria, which delayed the remittance of the money to the college. Since it took so long and nothing was known about the reason for the delay, I had assumed that the money might never come, so I wanted to replace it on my own. I had already earned the money I needed. When the bank money finally came, I used a part of it to buy a small used car, a Gremlin, paying cash for it. This was nice. A car made my life so much easier to get to where I wanted in time instead of using buses. I always got lost driving since I did not know my way around. I had to give myself extra time to get to wherever I needed to go. Shortly after I got the car, it had tire problems. I took it to Goodyear Tires to be checked and fixed. It cost $500.00 to fix the tires. When I went to pay and pick the car up, the mechanic asked me for a credit card. I did not know what a credit card was. In my culture, owing was frowned upon, it was disgraceful to owe, so I said to him, "Why are you so proud about owing? It is not nice to owe! I am going to pay cash." The mechanic looked at me like, "What is wrong with you, what planet are you from?" Looking very surprised, he said, "Okay, I am sorry. I did not mean to offend you." I paid him the five hundred dollars in cash and took my car back home.

That fall semester ended well, my grades were good. I continued working the same schedule in the nursing home in spite of the extra money that came in. I was qualified as a Registered Nurse and Midwife in Nigeria, so I checked with the Massachusetts State Board of Nursing to see what was required of me to earn an RN license in Massachusetts. They wanted to contact my nursing school directly to find out what we covered in the nursing program and to ascertain that I had attended an approved nursing school in Nigeria. They would not accept this information from me personally even though I had my transcript with me. I was happy when the state board of nursing confirmed that I had attended an approved nursing program in Nigeria and all the courses I took were accepted here in Massachusetts. I was then allowed to take the State Board of Nursing Exam without any further requirements. Oh! This felt so, so, good!

I put in for the State Board of Nursing Exam right away without any review. I was very impatient, so I relied on my nursing background from Nigeria. I failed the first and second attempts. This was my first academic failure so far in life. After my second failure, I realized that my weakness was in Psychiatric Nursing. I bought a psych textbook to study before trying again. During my second attempt, by chance, I ran into my nursing schoolmate from Nigeria taking the same exam in Boston. I was so surprised to see someone from my nursing school in Nigeria here in Boston. We were really excited and happy to meet again. At this time, the Nursing State Board Exam used to be held in Boston for all Massachusetts's candidates. This former nursing schoolmate had taken the exam a couple of times unsuccessfully. She advised me to take the LPN exam first, so that if I passed, I could start working as an LPN instead of as a nurse's aide. She told me that she thought that the LPN (License Practical Nursing) exam was easier than the RN exam. I took her advice and took the LPN exam. I went straight from work to take this exam in Boston. I did not have the time to reach home to freshen up and eat. Funny enough, I thought it was such a straightforward exam compared to the RN exam. I walked out of that exam hall believing that I passed. For me meeting my nursing schoolmate was a miracle and I thanked the Lord for it. The result of the LPN Exam came out and I was not surprised that I passed. I was happy and thankful for this progress. At work, my title was changed from nurse's aide to LPN and my pay and responsibilities were changed to reflect my changed status. They did not switch the nursing home unit, which I had worked on. This helped me a lot, since I was familiar with this unit including the patients, my co-workers, and the routine. I continued working full time at night and going to school, then I attempted the State Board of Nursing Exam the third time for the RN and I finally passed in March of 1981. It felt really good and I was thankful to the Lord for this. Many professionals who came from other countries to America that could not pass their board exams had to work in other areas. Some may be unlucky to lose their professions permanently. I have met many doctors and nurses who ended up working as a nurse's aide for this reason. I stayed on the same floor to work. By this time, I was completing my Bachelor's Degree in Public Health and had my RN license. I felt the reward of hard work and not giving up when things got tough, that led to my success. I was thankful to the Lord and humbled by His blessing. I had renewed confidence and courage to move on.

CHAPTER 16

The Answered Prayer

In March of 1980, when I had been living in the U.S for about a year, I received a letter from the young man from the bank at Calabar, Nigeria. He was the one who helped me with the foreign exchange transaction before I left for the U.S, when the woman who was supposed to help me walked out. He also was the one who gave me his name and address on a piece of folded paper as I was leaving the bank that day, which I then tore and threw away because I was leaving the country. I thought I would have nothing else to do with him after that day.

In his letter, he was asking for my hand in marriage. What! Is he crazy? I only met him that one day in the bank. I was so angry. I gave the letter to my nephew to read as I was ranting in my anger saying, "I don't know him; I only met him that one day in the bank and that was it. His father was my patient for two weeks on my hospital unit and he was still there when I left the hospital. I never noticed this man visiting his own father in the hospital. This does not make any sense to me." My nephew who is a very cool and soft-spoken person read the letter and said to me, "Enoh, this man is serious. I am being honest with you as a man, and I could see you with him as your future husband." Oh! I was so mad and I took it out on my nephew. "Is that how marriage works? Meet a total stranger; have no clue about his family background. I don't know what town or village he is from, and you are talking marriage? I think that is a disaster waiting to happen instead of a marriage." I snatched the letter from his hand and tore it into pieces as I was ranting and fuming in anger, throwing it into the trash and saying, "That's where this kind of marriage ends up." That was it for me! I tossed this thought out of my mind. Besides, I was too busy to pay attention to things like that and I did not reply to his letter.

About three months after the first letter, a second letter came. In this one, the man from the bank asked if I received his first letter because he never received a reply from me. He just wanted to know if I would marry him or not. He said he needed a reply either way, yes or no, to make a decision. If I said no, then he would look for another lady to marry. This second letter came during the summer vacation; I was taking some part time courses at another college. I was still working, but it was a lot less stressful, so I was a bit more tolerant. It was then that I remembered my special order to God for my future life partner "AT THE RIGHT TIME." I had written seven attributes that my future husband should have:

(1)   He must be a God fearing born again Christian. I felt then that if he was a born again Christian, we

will make it in our marriage under any circumstance, for better or worse.

(2)   He has to be a man of action and few words. I could not stand men who talked a lot. I thought then that it was all right for women to be talkers.

(3)   He must love and respect his parents. A man who loved and respected his parents most likely is going to love and respect his wife.

(4)   For me not to have a hand in the choice. If I were to choose a life partner, humanly speaking, I would go for handsomeness and wealth and these two may not hold my marriage together. If it were God's choice for me, He would give me His best. There was no divorce in this plan, so this man has to be God sent for me.

(5)   Physical appearance, I just had this image of how my future husband was going to look like, very specific facial features. He must be taller than me since I am a very petit woman.

(6)   He must speak the language my parents would understand. For this reason, I had already made up my mind that I would not marry outside my tribe since every state in Nigeria spoke a different language. I did not want to have an interpreter for my parents when my husband visited them. The funniest thing about this was, I rarely stayed in my state, and there was a higher chance for me to meet a man somewhere else.

(7)   I must have my parents' blessings to marry whoever he would be. If my parents rejected the one presented to them that would be it. I felt like my parents had enough life experience to guide me and would always wish the best for me. Their input in this vital decision was very important to me.

I had listed the seven things I wanted in my future husband back when I first started at nursing school in Nigeria. I had the list posted on my nightstand and prayed about it for the three and a half years that I was in nursing school. When I was done with that school, I tore the list and threw it away, believing that the Lord would give me who was best for me at the right time. I left the decision in God's hands and never worried about it again. When my mom told me her concern about my finding a husband, as I was ready to leave for America, I told her to rest assured that the Lord would provide all my needs including a husband in His perfect timing. Therefore, when this man's second letter came, I was able to think things through more calmly and clearly. Then I remembered what I had asked of the Lord several years ago. "Hmm, this may be him." I could not be sure. I replied to his second letter just listing the seven things I wanted in my future husband. I did not say yes or no to his proposal. "If you meet my criteria then you are the one," I thought. I mailed the letter to him. Letter writing was the primary means of communication then.

I then learned that when he received my letter, he visited my parents in the company of his aunt to ask for my hand in marriage. My sister Alice wrote me to ask me about him. She wrote, "This young man came one Sunday after-noon in the company of an elderly woman to ask your hand in marriage. You never gave us any hint that you had some-body for marriage; we were all surprised to see him. Secondly, you are in America and he is here in Nigeria. How is that going to work?"

I was so surprised! I could not wrap my head around this; I did not know what to do. I wrote back to my sister, trying to explain the situation and what happened. I then wrote my sis-ter again, and a couple of my close friends at home to "check him out" for me. I was surprised to receive positive feedback from my family and friends. They told me where he was from, that both his parents were still alive and that they had nine children, three boys and six girls. He was the second oldest child and he had an older brother. Once I received this infor-mation, I wrote him saying, if things did work out - which would he prefer? To have me come back to settle down with him in Nigeria or for him to come over to join me here in the U.S. He replied and said he would like to join me here in the U.S. I wanted to know so that we could plan. At this point, I asked him to send me his photograph to refresh my memory of him, which he did. It was a passport sized black and white photo of him in his afro cut hairstyle. I have always kept this photograph safely as I want it to be enclosed in my casket when I die.

I had already planned to visit Nigeria in the summer of 1981. I wanted to go home to see my parents who were getting older and weaker and to deal with the fact that I could lose any one of them before my next home visit. I also wanted to go check on the possibility of getting married; to see if it was God's will for me. I made all the preparations to fly from Boston to New York, and then take the international flight, PANAM, from New York to Lagos, Nigeria. The international flight was late to arrive in Lagos on Friday, so I missed the local flight to Calabar in my state. As a result, I had to spend a night in a hotel in Lagos. Instead of arriving at the local airport in Calabar on Friday evening, I arrived on Saturday morning about 9:30 am. I had informed my "prospective husband-to-be" of the time I was arriving so he had been at the Calabar airport on Friday evening waiting to pick me up and I was nowhere to be found. I had no means of informing him of my missed flight.

When I arrived Saturday morning, my relative and her husband were waiting to pick me up at the airport. I was so happy to see them. This was of great significance to me because they were the only people that saw me off when I left Nigeria and here they were again to welcome me back. I was grateful to them and emotional about it too. They took me to their house where I ate, took a bath and freshened up before both of them took me to my parents' home. Their hospitality, kindness, generosity and the fact that they were the people by which coming to America became a reality for me, for these reasons I will never forget them. I had bought memorable gifts for them and their children from the U.S. I did not know where life was going to drift us to, so this was my opportunity to thank them, and I did that to my satisfaction. When we arrived home, mom was ecstatic to see us; she would not let them go until she cooked for them. They stayed and had supper with us before they left. It felt right to me for my relative and her husband to have picked me up from the airport and brought me home to my parents instead of my "prospective husband-to-be." I think it would have been awkward if he had picked me up from the airport, since we were still strangers to each other. I thanked God for missing the local flight the previous evening.

My family had gathered at our house to welcome me back. It was so nice to see my parents as well as my sisters, nieces and nephews. They all stayed until that evening before they went to their own houses. I slept with my mom that night. It was so nice because I had missed her so much, and so we could talk late into the night. One of the hot topics we talked about was, "My man." I asked mom what she thought of him, not worrying about whatever answer she was going to give me. She said she liked him and she was giving me her blessing to marry him, if things worked out. Mom expressed her surprise that he just walked in without any notice from him and no hint from me that I had someone in my life. I told her that God works in mysterious ways. I shared with her as much as I could about the big and the small miracles the Lord had done for me, even up to opening the doors to America and help-ing me adjust to life within a different culture. I completely trusted and relied on God in all my undertakings even when it did not make sense to me at times. I shared with mom that "my man" could be one of the big miracles too. I narrated how the relationship started to where we were right then, and I was coming home to fulfil God's promise to me, that He would provide all my needs, even a husband at the right time. When I woke up the following morning, I couldn't believe this is real, I am home with my parents! Yes, it was real and I was over-joyed to be back to see both my parents alive.

It was now Sunday morning and my "prospective-hus-band-to-be" had no idea if I had come back to Nigeria or not since he had expected me on Friday evening. Here I was at home with my parents and he was at Calabar, about a three-hour drive from me. There were no telephones in my village then so I had no means of communicating with him. I talked to my mom about this, that I wanted to visit him. I had no idea where he lived and I may not even recognize him if he was in a group. The easiest way to handle this was for me to go back to the bank where he was working, which was our first meeting place. I could only do that on Monday, since the bank was not opened on weekends. Luckily for me, a cousin of mine who worked in Calabar had visited our home in the village that weekend. He gave me a ride early Monday morning to Calabar. He took me to African Continental Bank (ACB) where "my man" was working and both of us got to meet him. He was very happy and surprised to see me. We hugged and I apologized for not arriving the previous Friday as expected. He said he was worried about my safety from such a long trip and now he was relieved that I had arrived safely. We could not talk much since he was still at work and the bank was very busy on a Monday morning. He gave my cousin his house address and told us when he would be finished with work. My cousin took me to his own house where I spent the rest of the day praying and trying to sort things out in my mind for this probable life's journey I could be taking.

At 5:30 PM, I was ready to be taken to "my man's" house by my cousin. When we got there, he was back from work. He was living with his grown up younger sister, Ekaete, who cooked supper for us. We ate, talked and made some plans. I told him that the main purpose of this visit to him was to let him know that I was home on vacation for two weeks only. I needed to give him that information so that we could plan accordingly. He told me then, that his father had just died the week I had arrived. That made me very sad. His father was the only person I knew in his family. He had been my patient at St. Margaret's Hospital in Calabar before I left for the U.S., the one who used to call me "Ama-Asi." I was surprised to see how strong "my man" was for losing his father the previous week. I gave him my condolences and complimented him on his strength and courage at such a difficult time. He said it was such a relief for him since his father was very sick for a long time. It was hard but he had to do what he needed to do to move on, he said. We planned when he would be coming to visit my family for the traditional marriage and when I was going to visit his family for the first time. Up until this point, I had not visited or known the rest of his family members. I had just two weeks' vacation. Since my now "husband-to-be" had already visited my parents earlier to ask my hand in marriage while I was still in the U.S., the following weekend, Saturday, his family would come to mine for the official traditional marriage ceremony. Then we were done with the planning and I had to go back home to my parents' house. I told my mom of all our plans and she approved.

With the situation we were both in, with him just losing his father and our planning to go back to the U.S the following week, my parents understood and did not bother to give them a list of what they would have expected my future in-laws to bring that Saturday. That was postponed to a future date when a situation was more conducive. The time for the marriage ceremony to start was 10:00 AM. My parents had invited other family members and some friends. My family cooked assorted foods and bought many drinks. My "in-laws-to-be" arrived on time and it was a very special occasion for me. My mother-in-law- to- be could not come, since she had just lost her husband the previous week. Up to this point, I had not met his mother and my mom did not want me to go back with them that Saturday. She wanted me to stay with her. Usually after the marriage ceremony, the new wife would follow the husband to his family according to the tradition. People ate and drank and there was a lot of fun. After all was said and done, my parents sat both of us down and advised us. They admonished us to live peacefully with each other since we were going to be so far from home with no one around to help us. My mom told my now husband that she would send me to him the following day. He was okay with that. We were done with the traditional marriage on that Saturday about 2:30 PM and my new husband and in-laws left without me, so I could spend extra time with my own family.

The following day, Sunday after church, my mom arranged for my oldest sister Mammie to escort me to my new husband's village to visit his family for the first time. There, we met with the rest of his family. We were warmly welcomed. His mother cooked for us and we had supper together. Then my sister left me with them and went back home to let my parents know her impression of his family. I was able to see where my husband was from and met his entire family. I felt at home with them. His family was so similar to mine that I felt very comfortable right away. His mom took me in and treated me as one of her children and I respected her as a mother. She told me that when she expressed her concern to her husband while he was still alive, over not having met me yet, he reassured her that I was a very lovely person. He also told her that she was going to love me. Yes, she did. My mother-in-law used to call me "Anie-Ama," which is translated "Love-Who-You-Have." I spent two days with them, then I had to bid them goodbye, knowing that I did not have the time to visit them again before we travelled back to the U.S.

By now, my new husband had received admission to a college in the U.S. Everything was ready for him to leave with me the following week. I thought to myself "Can this be true? Yes." This was a great miracle; my dream came true, to God's glory. America here we come! To start our lives together, not knowing each other. We studied and got to know each other in our marriage. The advantages I had in getting married to a man I did not know were:

(1) I got my wish. I did not want to have a hand in the choice of whom I was going to marry. I left that to God, knowing that His choice would be the best for me.

(2) We did not take each other for granted from the get-go.

(3) There were no flowery illusions "in the name of love," and the pretense and deceit, love is blind kind of stuff.

(10) It worked for me and it may not work for everyone. I thank the Lord for answering my prayer.

In all, 1981 was a very memorable year for me. It was the year I passed my Board of Nursing exam to become a registered nurse and earned my bachelor's degree in Health and Human Services. I visited my family in Nigeria that summer, got married and came back to the U.S with my brand new husband. I became pregnant that summer and started my Master's Degree in Nursing in the fall of that year. I was a very happy woman. I was thankful to God for all His blessings and more so for the opportunity I had to see my parents once again. That ended up being the last time I ever saw my dad alive. He died in 1984.

CHAPTER 17

Our New Life in America

I returned from the two- week summer vacation with my new husband. When we came back to the U.S, my husband registered at his college for a Bachelor's Degree in Financial Management while I started my Master's Degree in Nursing in the fall of that year, 1981. He got a job and we were both working fulltime and going to college. For the Master's Graduate program, attending classes two evenings a week was considered fulltime compared to five days a week for the Bachelor's degree. The class time was longer in the master's program, three hours per class time as opposed to one hour in the Bachelor's program. This was less hectic for me compared to my previous class schedule in the Bachelor's program. I appreciated the ease it gave me and it was a great relief. I did not want any more stress in my life at this time.

Then I realized I was pregnant with my first baby. I felt really good and healthy throughout my pregnancy. I had never had health insurance before because I thought it was too expensive for me to afford. At this point, I needed to buy private health insurance in order to be covered for the rest of my pregnancy and after delivery. This being my first pregnancy, it did not show until I was about seven months. Once I started showing, I just grew fast. I was teased in college by my friends that I was going to have the baby right in class one of these days. I used to tell them that since I was a midwife, I would help conduct my own delivery and that I had my emergency delivery kit handy. We all laughed about it. I completed most of my classes, knowing that the baby was coming soon. In preparation for the baby, all I had left to do were a few last courses and my graduate thesis. I kind of figured that I would have more time to enjoy my baby while doing the research for my graduate program.

My nephew's girlfriend who went back to Nigeria in 1979 revisited him in the fall of 1981, here in America. She was surprised to see my progress. Before while she was here, I was brand new in America, I was trying to find my way, and I was clueless. Maybe she thought I was going to stay that way forever. No! I learned and I grew in all aspects of my life. During this visit, she was shocked to see that I had my own car; I had earned a bachelor's degree and was doing my master's degree in Nursing. I was married and expecting our first baby. Oh! That was too much for her to take in. It felt so good to have achieved so much in two years of being in America.

My first pregnancy was great, I felt really good and energized. Feeling good, I did not anticipate any problem with my delivery, I totally forgot that being a petit woman and I could have cephalopelvic disproportion, which means that my pelvic cavity was too small for the head of my baby to fit in or be engaged. In my last month of pregnancy, the Braxton Hicks contractions increased in intensity and frequency, which was normal. One Saturday night, I was up finishing a course assignment, when I stood up to use the bathroom; I felt some fluids running down my legs. Oops, did I just pee on myself? I went to the bathroom to discover that it was amniotic fluid (my water was leaking). I called the hospital and was told to come in right away. I woke my husband up and we arrived at the hospital about 5:30 AM. I was checked and admitted into the Labor and Delivery Unit, but I was not in active labor yet. A couple of hours later, my "real labor" contractions started. It was good that I was able to have a few hours of sleep in the hospital before my labor started, since I had been awake most of that previous night doing my college coursework. I needed that extra rest. I was in active labor for 8 hours without any progress. The doctor ordered intravenous fluids for me since I was not allowed to eat or drink anything. The fetal monitor was connected to check on the baby's welfare. I was being monitored closely, but I was not progressing. Here I was observing all that was going on as a registered nurse and a midwife, yet I did not tell any of the hospital staff about my nursing background. In one of the questions somewhere in my chart, I was asked what I did for a living and I had told them that I was a housewife. My rationale for saying that was; I wanted to be a patient and to be treated as such. I did not want any of the healthcare providers assuming that I already knew everything and then not give me all the information and care I needed.

Watching the fetal monitor, my baby was doing all right but I was getting tired. My baby's head was still not engaged, so I opted for a Caesarian Section. They wanted to prolong the labor to see if I could deliver the baby naturally, but I declined that option. Then they wanted to call first and notify my husband and ask him to come in and sign the consent form. I said, "I will sign the consent form now, then you can notify my husband of the surgery." I had a strong feeling of urgency to get the baby out. It did not matter to me, "how," but to make sure I had a healthy baby. They gave me the consent form, which I signed; I was given a spinal anesthesia and taken in for an emergency Caesarian Section. With the spinal anesthesia, I was awake, but did not have any sensation on the lower part of my body. The nurse inserted a foley catheter in me, in the operating room before the surgery started. There was a drape over me so that I could not see what the surgeon was doing. When the baby was delivered, he cried loudly, I was thrilled and emotional to hear my baby's first cry! They showed him to me, oh! He was so handsome and sweet. The magic of new life is indescribable. The baby was cleaned up, suctioned and wrapped in a warm blanket. By this time, my husband had arrived to see our newborn baby boy.

I had an uneventful recovery. The nurses, obstetrician and the nurse's aide were great professionals. I was impressed with them all. I thanked them on my discharge and then told them that I was a nurse and a midwife. They were surprised that I did not disclose this information earlier and wrote it in my chart. This was the first time I had been hospitalized in my entire life.

I derived my research topic for the thesis in my master's graduate program from that first experience as a patient when I had my first baby. The topic was, "Patient View of Their Hospitalization." It was an eye-opener to be a patient after working as a nurse for seven years prior. There are many ways being a patient has influenced my clinical practice for good. It has made me more empathetic to my patients, increased my sensitivity to patient needs and a quicker response time. It also made me more aware of how restrictive, powerless, helpless and embarrassed ill heath can render anybody. Sickness is no respecter of persons, the young, old, rich and poor. Even doctors and nurses get sick. The conclusion of my research work was that if all healthcare workers were patients at some point in their practice, it would have a positive outcome both for them and for their patients.

I had two more children after that and my subsequent deliveries were done by elective Caesarian Section by my choice. I was given an option for trial labor with my second baby but I declined. With my physical size, it was easier for me to have an elective Caesarian Section than go through a probable failed trial. After my second child, a baby girl, as I was leaving the maternity unit, a couple of the nurses said to me, "That's it for you, you have a boy and a girl," and I said, "No, I am coming back again." I did come back one more time and

I had another girl. When my husband brought the two older children to visit me and the new baby in the hospital, my son who was six years old then, noticed that the new baby was a girl. He was very upset. He had his arms folded, stepped away from me and said, "Oh no, this is not the right order of things. You had my sister and me. This baby is supposed to be a boy, my brother, not another girl! Leave her here at the hospital and make sure you bring home a boy, my brother." I did not expect this reaction from him. I realized then that he thought babies came in order: boy, girl, boy, girl, so he was expecting a boy, his brother. I pulled him over to give him a big hug and told him not to worry, that his baby sister was going to grow up to be the best little sister to him in the whole world. Yes, she has grown up to be very close to him. Today my son is a grown up man with three children of his own, two boys and a girl in the middle. My granddaughter complained to me that it was not fair that the new baby was a boy; she thought her mom was going to give her a sister. I hugged her and said to her, "He is going to be the best little brother in the whole world." She smiled and said, "I hope so." Her little brother is about six years old as I am writing this, and she loves him.

CHAPTER 18

My Life as a Wife, Mother, Full-Time Student, and a Professional

Looking back, it is amazing how my husband and I have navigated through life this far given the fact that we started out together as total strangers to each other. I thought we did not know each other, but apparently, while his father was my patient in the hospital at Calabar, my husband used to visit him a lot. He came in frequently, to observe me unnoticed while I was at work. He told me this after we were married and were here in the U.S. He said he was impressed by his father's good comments about me. This drew his attention to me. Well, my patient, his father, had always had many guests, and I never noticed any of them since I was only focused on my patient. I believed my husband when he recounted an occasion that he and his siblings visited their father and I came to attend to his father and I politely asked them to wait outside the patient's room. Once I finished what

I had to do with my patient, I came back to call them in to visit with their father. I remember that occasion, but I did not pay any attention to the visitors. I did not even notice whether they were male, female or children. From this account, he knew me sort of, but I met him for the first time in the bank at Calabar as I was getting ready to leave for the U.S.

We were married and started a family right away, no time to loose! Both of us were going to college and working fulltime. We had very little time for each other, but we both understood what we wanted and needed in life, so we just had to go for it. It was amazing that we knew where one left off; the other would take over without words. I still do not understand how we cultivated this habit, but it helped us in staying connected and respectful to each other. There was no room and time for bickering and fighting with each other. We were both too busy and knew what we wanted in life and we had each other's back.

There is no "school" that really teaches you how to adjust to life, you just have to figure out what works for you, and what works for you may not work for other people. Since both my husband and I were college students and working full time, I decided to continue working nights. In doing so, when the children came, it was easier for my husband to watch them at night while I worked, then I was with my children during the day. Once I came home from work about 7:15-7:30 AM, I would get the kids ready and drop them off at their schools. When I got back home, I would eat, shower and go to bed, getting up to pick them up from school at 2:00

PM. Once they got home from school, they would eat and do their homework, which would take them until about 4:00 PM. After homework, I would take them for playtime outside in a park if the weather was conducive or anywhere they could play safely until about 6:00 PM. When we would come back home, I would give them supper, baths and everybody including me was in bed by 7:00 PM EST. This was the time I got the bulk of sleep to carry me through the night at work, and the children would not miss me since they were sleeping during the time I went into work. When the children were older, they were able to wake up and be ready for school, so when I drove in from work, they were ready to be dropped off to their schools. During summer vacations, I would take them to the park from about 8:00 to 10:00 AM to play while I walked to get some exercise during the cool mornings. Weekends and winter vacation, I would keep them at home until between 2:00-3:00 PM and then take them outside for playtime. This routine continued as my children grew older.

I was still working at the bedside, taking care of the patients on the hospital units with a master's degree in Nursing, which I earned shortly after I had my second baby. I decided to take a break from going for a PhD in Nursing, right away to take care of my young children. I told my husband then that I would go back to school when the children are grown and out of the house. "It may be easier then," I thought. I talked this over with my husband and he said to me, "Enoh, keep going, you are doing well so far. If you stop now, it may be hard to go back to school in the future. I will help you with the children." He helped me find a graduate school right away, which both of us applied to, and we were accepted. Two months after we started in the program, I became pregnant with my third child. I refused to quit, I kept going and completed my PhD in Nursing a year after I had my third and last baby. I was very happy that I did not quit or take a break. I thanked my husband for his encouragement to get my PhD in Nursing. He was supportive of me and the children throughout this period and he had always been there for us 100 percent.

I kept the same schedule, doing the same thing a couple of years after I had my Ph.D. It paid off as I was able to balance both home and work with a lot less stress, enjoyed my children and was able to be there for them all the way. It made me feel really good to have this balance both at home and at work. My son played in basketball and baseball leagues; I never missed any of his practices or games. My two daughters were both involved in gymnastics as an out of school activity, sports and music in school. I also had time for both of them. One of the great things about being a nurse was the flexibility of my work hours. Working nights made me free all day, so I was always there for my children - sometimes tired and sleepless, which is part of being a mother. Looking back, I am thankful to God for directing my life so that I do not have any regrets about the past. I was able to juggle it all in a satisfactory way for me. It was not easy, but it was worth it all in the end.

In my career as a nurse in the U.S., I worked in nursing homes, local hospitals and nursing agencies. In one of the local hospitals where I worked, a nursing supervisor or administrative coordinator's position was available. I applied and obtained the job after I had worked there for many years, taking care of the patients. This made me extremely happy. My new position was to cover the whole hospital on nights, for staffing, dealing with any issue that came up in any of the hospital units. I could handle this position at this time since my children were older and they were all in school. My pay was increased with the new position, but it was not sufficient for my added financial responsibility at home. My son was almost finished with high school at this time and I had no money saved for his college yet. I decided to try other ways to make additional income to meet this need.

I joined a financial services company. We were trained on how to make money by helping people get out of debt quicker. My husband told me not to waste my time and energy in it but the business sounded so good to me and I could not resist it. I joined, giving myself a year to try it. If it worked, I would continue, if it did not work out I would quit. I was going to help people —and in doing so, make some extra money. It was going to be a win- win situation. I enjoyed the business, but was not making as much money as we were promised. We went to their conference in Georgia, which was held in the Georgia "Dome." It was a big place and many people attended. They had many motivational speakers delivering on how they became rich through this company. I sat listening to them and thinking, "Could this be me one day?" I was still evaluating the success of this business after the conference. It was almost a year later and I did not see it succeeding.

A week after we came back from Georgia, I was supposed to apply for my financial security license, when Becker College called me on a Monday, for a position to head a new International Nursing Program. This program was designed to help foreign-trained nurses transition to American nursing since there was a nursing shortage here in the U.S. I asked the caller when I could come in to find out more about this position. She told me to come in on Wednesday at 10:00 AM. I went in on that Wednesday just to get more information; instead, I was offered the job, which I accepted. I was very pleased with this. I had come to America as an international nurse and had nobody to guide me. I did not even know where to find resources to help me. I felt this was God's way of allowing me to help nurses from other countries who would come here to the U.S. to find their way more easily than I did. This made me very happy to know I could help others in a similar situation.

I was sent to Human Resources to fill out paperwork for the hiring. This took place in the summer of 2001; I was expected to start work in the fall of that year. I was given the list of each of the nurses accepted into the program and their various countries. When fall classes started, the international nurses never came. The college informed me that there were some logistical problems and they were still working on it. The foreign nurses not coming may have had something to do with the terrorist attack of 9/11/2001 in the U.S. While waiting, I was offered an Adjunct Nursing Faculty position at the same college, which I accepted. What the college offered me for pay was enough for my son's tuition in college that semester. This was a miracle; I was ecstatic and very thankful to God. With this new direction, I had no need for the financial service business. God had answered my prayers. I stayed with the college and taught as par-time adjunct Nursing Faculty for the next four years. I then let the college know that I would be available to teach fulltime in the spring of the following year. They gave me more hours as an adjunct Nursing Faculty in the fall of that semester. I was so thankful to the Lord for all His blessings on me. I was interviewed and was hired as a full Professor to start the following spring semester. As an adjunct faculty, I was mentored into my teaching role and was given the opportunity to observe other professors' lectures. I was also asked to do a couple of lectures under observation and continued doing clinical instruction in the local hospital for the college. I liked the college a lot. It did not take me long to realize that this was it for me career wise. Right there and then, I knew that I would work for this college until my retirement.

My life as a fulltime Professor started in the spring of 2005. The semester before, I was oriented to the teaching role. This was very important for me when I started teaching fulltime; I was comfortable in my new position. The first class I taught was Nursing 2 for the second semester students in the Associate Degree Nursing (ADN) Program at Becker College. In the fall of 2005, I taught Health Assessment until the spring of 2010. Then I was switched to teach the Fundamentals of Nursing class from the fall of 2010 to the spring of 2017. In the fall of 2015, the Bachelor of Science in

Nursing (B.S.N) Fundamentals class was added to the ADN Fundamentals class I was already teaching. My workload also included labs for different nursing levels, teaching clinical in nursing homes, subacute and critical care settings for different nursing levels. As a full time Professor, I could have opted not to do clinical instruction, but I did not. I love teaching my students in class, labs and clinical. The privilege of having students in all three areas gave me the continuity to assess my students' progress, build on their strengths, and support their weaknesses. I also appreciated the hands on in the clinical settings since it kept me current in my clinical practice and caring for my patients. I am very flexible; I prefer to have different classes or clinical levels each semester. I like to switch around since each nursing level is handled differently. Teaching in all the different areas of nursing made it easy for me to fill in for others, if there was any need or emergency. The lectures, labs and clinical enhanced each other and the students gained more knowledge and understanding through the combination of these three areas. The lab and clinical are hands- on. This gives each student nurse an opportunity to start practicing under the supervision and guidance of an instructor while they are exposed to the art and science of nursing. By the time a student nurse has graduated, he/she has acquired the skills and knowledge to start practicing in the real world. All health care settings have an orientation program for new graduates to ease them into clinical practice.

It is extremely rewarding to be a part of molding the beginners into future nurses. The depth of appreciation and gratitude of my students is priceless to me. In nearly every health care setting I have visited, I always find nurses that I have taught when they were students. They all remember me. I remember some of them, especially if I had them in class, lab and clinical or if they were my advisees. There are higher chances that I may not remember them if I only had them in class for lectures, since I had many students in my class. Oh, the joy of seeing the progress of my students in the nursing profession is immeasurable! Right now, my direct boss at Becker College was also my former student. I do work with many full time and adjunct faculty members that were my former students too. To have played a part in helping to produce future nursing professionals is my pride. Oh, how sweet it is!

My dream of working for Becker College until I retire came true in the fall of 2017. I started working for the College in the fall 2001. I will continue to work as a retired adjunct Nursing Faculty for my college until I cannot do it anymore. It is a great place to work and I have been blessed to be a part of this awesome institution. I was shocked and humbled to be given the "Award for Excellence in Teaching" in the 2013-2014 academic year. In addition, in the fall of 2017, I started to work as a retired adjunct Nursing Faculty for Anna Maria College. This was the first College I attended for my Bachelor's degree when I arrived in the United States of America.

CHAPTER 19

Introduction of Computerized Documentation in Nursing

The introduction of computers in the healthcare system caught me by surprise. In my bachelor's program in the late seventies and early eighties, I was required to take a course in computer programing. By then the computerized system had not permeated the whole world as it has today. It meant nothing to me then. I took it because it was a required course. I just tried to get a "C" to pass it so I did not need to repeat the class. I thought I was done with computers after taking this course and passing it. No! More was coming.

Newness is never easy. You have to try to figure out what is new by studying it, asking questions and doing research and the more you are exposed to newness, the more comfortable you become. Before you know it, you are becoming more comfortable and growing. When newer people come into school or the work place, and see you as an experienced nurse, they are asking you questions and you realize how far you have come.

This make you remember your own beginnings. Wherever you have reached in your dreams, do not ever forget where you started from and do not treat the beginners as if they do not know anything. Respect them. They too will get there and may even go further and do better than you do. Some people think that newness and changes are always difficult and uncomfortable. Yes, that is true, but you cannot progress in life without stepping out of your comfort zone to try something new, where you can learn, grow and acquire new skills. It is nerve racking at the beginning but with time and practice, you can end up being an expert in your field of practice.

In the local hospital where I was working in Worcester, all documentation then was by pen and paper, black or blue colored pen on days, green on evenings and red on nights. That was how it was then, in many health care setting. One day in this local hospital, they had rented a robot for a trial to run errands. The name of the robot was Chet. What? A robot to run errands? I guess it did not work out or for some reason; it was not brought on board after the trial period. A couple of years after Chet, there was the introduction of computerized documentation of certain parts of patient care, starting with medication administration. Before I realized it, there was the introduction of complete computerized documentation of patient care, first in the acute care setting, "COMPUTERS ON WHEELS-COW."

The long-term care setting took a lot longer to catch on to the new wave of computers in the healthcare industry. In the beginning, I lived through the introduction and full use of computerized documentation of patients' care. We all had to be trained. I struggled with going back and forth between paper and computerized documentation since I did clinical and some part time jobs in facilities that were still using paper documentation. Changing from paper to computer documentation was hard, but once I had the hang of it, I felt it was a lot better than paper documentation. Some people actually quit their jobs during the introductory phase of computerized documentation in the healthcare setting. They thought it was too frustrating and they were never going to get it. I do not know how far they ran, all I know is, you will not outrun computer documentation in the health care industry. It is here to stay. Computers were provided for all the healthcare providers; nurses were provided with computers to take to the patient's bedside to document care as it was being given.

In my opinion, the introduction of computers into the healthcare system is great; it has really enhanced the delivery of patient care, reduced error, improved communication, saved time and increased patient and staff satisfaction.

CHAPTER 20

Forgiveness

For thirty-five years, I was very angry with my brother and his wife for the abuse they put me through as a child while I was living with them. However, I still visited them whenever I could in spite of how I felt about them. Once I was on my own after graduating from the midwifery school, I made a decision never to eat or drink from my brother's house for the rest of my life. This stemmed from when I was a helpless child; I was starved every day by my brother's wife, not because they did not have food. I still do not understand why she did this to me. When I was older, I could afford whatever I wanted and when I visited them, they always offered me food. I said, "No, thanks." They did not care when I needed it most, why should I bother to eat at their house now? I decided that I would keep to that; nothing would change my mind about this even after I had forgiven them. There was nothing they could have given me that I cannot afford for myself now. I even helped them out financially during my years living in the United States of America.

Whenever my brother and his wife were brought up in any conversation, I would feel this great anger welling up within me and spilling out. Just thinking about them made me very angry. This continued until one day in church, the minister's topic was on forgiveness. I had heard preaching on this topic many times before, but it did not cut it for me. This particular Sunday, I believed the Lord sent this message directly to me. The minister said, "It is you who have not forgiven that is carrying the burden on yourself. The people you are angry with may not even realize that you are angry with them." He continued by saying, "The message of forgiveness is given to you today to act on it. This will release you from that burden and give you peace. Go to whoever offended you right after this service, talk things over and forgive them. It will be a great relief for you. If you cannot meet these people, call them or write to let them know that you have forgiven them." I received the message very clearly for the first time, with my brother and his wife in mind. I was totally broken on how the Lord sent that message to me. I cried that day in church and for the first time, I truly forgave my brother and his wife for all they had done to me as a child.

I made plans to go home to Nigeria in the summer of 1996, solely to mend things with my brother and his wife. I brought a lot of presents and money to them. I took that opportunity to thank them for bringing me up without any anger or bitterness. I was truly appreciative of them at this time. As hard as it was then living such a terrible life as a child, it has actually molded me into who I am today-a strong, independent, hard worker and a go-getter who knows when to stand up for myself irrespective of the consequences. It made me very appreciative of people and life itself. I do not take anything for granted knowing what it felt like to be poor, deprived, oppressed, and demeaned unnecessarily, when I was growing up. By the grace of God, my tough time in my brother's house never affected my self-image; instead, it made me stronger and more self-reliant.

I find that forgiveness is a strength and not a weakness. Many times, it draws the forgiver and the forgiven even closer. I continued to help my brother and his wife financially while they were alive and then helped their children with their burial. Today, when people hurt me, I pay them back with kindness and love.

CHAPTER 21

Reflections

I have enjoyed being a nurse so much that I cannot put a price on it. It is now that I truly understand "My calling to be a Nurse." I almost missed that call due to my human nature and lack of understanding but the Lord redirected me to the righces of healthcare setting for over 40 years.

(1)   Due to my first experience with death in the health care settings, I am very careful today when my students experience a patient's death for the first time. I gently work them through the dying process and then ask the students who are not scared to help me with post mortem care of the body. Some of the students can just watch without touching the body and some may not even want to see the body. This is okay at first, I know with time my students too, will overcome their fear of death. Some of my clinical groups would request to visit the mortuary in the hospital; I always honor their request and take them

there. I understand that nurses help the sick get better but similarly, they help the sick die peacefully when death is inevitable and imminent. You cannot escape dealing with death and dying as a nurse, as scary as it may be at first.

(2) When I have a goal, I do not allow anything to stop me from achieving it. For example, in my second semester in college, on the first day of class, one of my professors came into class. As she walked in, she said, pointing to me, "You, leave my class." I stood up and said to her, "I need this class for my course." Then she said to me, "You leave my class now, you don't belong here." It was then that I understood that she did not want me in her class, since I was the only black student, which was the case in most of my classes then in the late seventies and early eighties. I then sat down and the rest of the students were just looking at each other since they all heard this professor order me out of her class. She then gave out a printed handout and introduced the course. The student sitting next to me on my right did not know what to do when it was her turn to pass the handout to me. She held it and I said to her, "Excuse me," and I took the handout from her, took mine and then passed the rest of the handouts to the student on my left. I think it was at this point that the whole class and my professor knew that I was not leaving, as I was demanded to do so. I sat through that lecture and after the class; I went to the Director of Nurses for the college and told her what hap-

pened. She gave me a hug and said she would look into it. Yes, she did look into it because a different professor taught that class for the rest of the semester. I never saw that professor again, or I may have encountered her without recognizing her. I blocked her out of my mind and I got an A in that class.

(3) In nursing, you come across many people with different personalities, attitudes and beliefs. I always maintain respect while explaining the situation so that this person can understand. A professor in college asked me "What language do you think in?" "Hmmm, I do not have a thinking language but I have expressive language," I answered her. When you speak one language only, you may think that you do your thinking in that language but, when you are multilingual, your thoughts have no language, you need a language to express your thought to the person you are talking to. This professor stood there, looking at me. Then I asked her why she asked me that question. She said that she thought I would form words and sentences in my native language in my mind and then translate it into English, since English is a second language for me. When people ask me questions like that, I do not get angry or annoyed. I realize they are learning too. We all learn from each other.

(4) I have always had a high value for education and I have encouraged my children, students and co-workers to continue in their education. The career mobility with furthering your education is very rewarding. I started

working as a nurse's aide in a nursing home when I first came to America. I was going to school for my bachelor's degree in Nursing, and I was trying to take the Massachusetts State Board of Nursing Exam on my own. When I succeeded in becoming an RN, I was still working on the same unit in the nursing home. I encouraged the nurses' aides that worked with me to go back to school to become nurses. Three out of the four of them went back to school. One of the three could not finish because of her home situation, she said. Two completed and became RNs. One of them refused to go back to school. One of them that became a nurse, Paula, is a very dear friend to this day. I still encourage people I encounter to further their education. The benefit outweighs the sacrifice.

(5) I never allow my patients' attitude to affect how I deliver care to them. They are sick and sometimes illness can bring the worst out of a good person. I had a patient in one of the local hospitals where I worked from 11:00 PM to 7:00 AM. After taking over from the evening nurse, I went in to see my patient and to introduce myself to him as his night nurse. He looked at me and said, "N-, don't touch me." I answered him and said, "Okay," and I left his room and went to tell my charge nurse to switch him and give me another patient, since my patient did not want me to take care of him that night. The charge nurse gave me a different patient. It was noted on his chart that he did not want me to take care of him, so I would not

be assigned to him again. However, each night before I went in to work, I would first go to say hi to him and ask how he was doing. Sometimes he answered me, other times he would give me a look like, "You again?" It didn't bother me whatever his response was. I kept stopping in to see him. His wife was there with him all the time. This patient was a medical doctor and he had a younger sister who was a nurse. She visited him occasionally. On this particular night when I came in to work, his wife asked me if I could do private home care for her husband. He was being discharged the following day. I said, "Oh yes, I can do that for you but did you check with your husband first?" "Yes," she said. I could not believe her, so I said, "Let's go check with the patient first." Both of us went in and asked him and he said yes. He was discharged the following day. I did private home care for him until his passing after three months. His wife and I remained friends afterwards.

(6)   It is always good to be professional and cordial to people. This does not mean that you let people walk all over you and treat you with disrespect. I had a patient that was visited by her daughter in the local hospital I worked. The daughter came in as I was attending to her mother. She asked me, "Are you the nurse aide?" I answered, "No." Then she asked me if I was an LPN. When I said no, she was upset. At this point, I said to her, "Why can't you ask me what I am? You just walked in to tell me what I should be and it is upsetting you because I am not what

you want me to be. Next time be sure to ask and don't just assume." She stomped out of her mother's room to ask another nurse on the unit who and what I was. When she found out that I was a registered nurse and had a master's degree in nursing, she never visited her mother again on my shift.

(7) I believe God answers prayer: I assigned a student to a male patient who was very sick at the local hospital where we were doing a clinical rotation. The patient's wife was always there with him. He was very depressed and emotional because of his health and his own father was dying of cancer. He wanted to be there for his father, but he was here in the hospital, ill in bed himself. I took the time to listen to him. When he was done with all he could say, I felt helpless and all I could do was to go to Jesus in prayer for my patient. In order not to push my spirituality on him, I asked him his religion. "I worship the God of Sun," he said. I asked, "May I pray with you please?" "Yes," he said. I started to pray saying, "Dear God of the sun, moon and stars, we your children are here seeking thy face and thy mercy..." Before I knew it, I was pleading with Jesus to forgive my patient, to grant him healing, and to give him peace. I was totally taken by the Holy Spirit as I was praying with him. After the prayer, I asked his nurse if my student nurse could take him out to the Atrium of the hospital. This is a very beautiful spacious area where there are many non-patient related activities going on. The nurse said yes. My student took

this patient to the Atrium for a short while and brought him back. Soon after they came back, two of his brothers who had not visited him during his hospitalization showed up. He was surprised and happy to see them. The following clinical day, I assigned him to the same student who had him previously. He had improved in his health and they were planning to discharge him before our next clinical day. He told me that day, "That he was now a changed man." He showed me his Bible and now he was at peace and he would go home a new man in Christ. This was beautiful and very emotional for me.

(8) I cannot explain why I have a strong inclination sometimes to follow up on some of my patients after they had been discharged home from the hospital. I had one of those patients. She was recovering well. I had visited her a couple of times, and called her over the phone just to make sure she was all right. I sent her a Christmas card that year, and her daughter whom I did not know, and had never met, sent me a note saying that her mother had passed. That made me very sad since I would have liked to attend her funeral.

(9) I believe in helping out whenever I can. One of my students was a single mother. She moved back home with her parents while she was in nursing school. She completed the program but couldn't afford the NCLEX (National Council Licensing Examination) fee. The Director of Nursing brought this student's problem to the faculty's attention. I volunteered to pay for her as her

anonymous donor. To my joy, she took the NCLEX and passed at her first attempt.

(10) My teaching role does not stop at the college as far as my students are concerned. Sometimes it takes me into their personal lives and their families. This is a letter from one of my students that I want to share with you with her permission:

> *Professor, I wanted to write you this to say thank you for everything you have done for me. I can honestly tell you that if it wasn't for you calling me last semester and encouraging me to go to class, I think I would have dropped out. After losing my fiancé on the second day of school my first semester of Nursing School, I was ready to run away. I will never forget the last call you made to me two days after we buried him. You told me that sitting at home crying and wallowing in self-pity would not help my future. That by sitting at home things would only get harder, and the spiral downhill would continue. At the time, I didn't want to go back. But I did. I went back the next day and scheduled all of my make up labs. I had my first exam the following week. I remember that I got an 88 on that test. You congratulated me and told me that when you saw my grade you wanted to cry because I still managed to make it out on top after all that was thrown my way. Well, here we are at the end of the first year and I made it through another semester. I can't*

tell you how grateful I am to have had you this last year to be my encouragement to push forward. I will never forget the phone calls you made to check up on me, to encourage me to get my butt to school, and the support you have given me this semester with the loss of my grandfather and my father being ill. I hope you see the immense impact you have made on all of us in this program. You have taught me so much more than I could ever put into words. Thank you for being you.

Sincerely-----Signed.

This student was, is, and will ever remain my "SHERO." She did very well in the Nursing Program and passed her Board of Nursing Exam (NCLEX) on her first attempt in spite of the tough times she went through in her life while in college. She is now happily married and moving on in her life.

(11) I realize that nursing school can be a difficult and confusing time for students; therefore, I give my students my private phone number to call me anytime they have questions or concerns out of class. I know that I could help them and lessen some of their frustration in my course. I got a call from one particular student. She was having a difficult time hearing heart and lung sounds and doing manual blood pressure. Their competency exam in the lab was coming up soon. I asked her when I could meet with her. There was no convenient time for

both of us besides class time since she had little children at home. I told her that she could bring her children to my house. She should also bring her blood pressure cuff and her stethoscope with her. When she got to my house, the first thing I did was to check for the patency of her stethoscope. The stethoscope was not patent or (turned on), this was why she could not hear the heart and lung sounds. I adjusted the stethoscope and tested it again for patency by putting the two earpieces in my ears and tapping lightly on the diaphragm. It was working now. I gave the stethoscope back to the student and then asked her to listen to my heartbeats. She was surprised to hear very clearly. I then showed her what the problem had been. She was very happy and then she did well in her lab competency test.

(12) As a professor, you would like to have a 100% pass rate in your class, but that is not always the case. Sometimes you definitely have students who are not doing well. To such students I try all I can to help them succeed. Unfortunately, by midterm, if these students have not improved, they tend to give up on themselves. Some of them may even withdraw from the college. When I encounter such students, the first thing I do is to give them hope, hope not to give up on themselves, followed by studying strategies. This works! One particular student was such a success story. I had helped her extensively before she took her final exam. The faculty nor-

mally had retention and progression meetings after final exams. In these meetings, each class coordinator would give a report on his or her class results. When this particular student's name came up, I learned she passed. I reacted in shock that she made it! I slumped down in my chair, hardly believed what I had heard and I went blank for a moment. When I recollected myself, I was so happy and emotional about this. I never saw this student until the beginning of the next semester. We ran into each other on campus. She couldn't wait to give me a hug. We stood in that embrace with tears of joy running down our faces. She thanked me repeatedly for being there for her.

I believe that in nursing school, failure is not fatal, as painful as it may feel to the student. It is another opportunity to re-learn and "Get it." Some of the students who still ended up failing and repeating in my class would come back to express how they did not realize how much they "Did not know" until after they had repeated the class. For my students to come to this realization is amazing. The pain, anger, frustration and humiliation of failure is finally put to rest since repeating a class makes for a stronger and better student, moving forward. Some knowledge is not optional for a nurse. Peoples' lives are in our hands and if it is necessary to repeat a class, there is no shame in that. The material is too important to leave without knowing it.

Here is a letter from one student:

(13)   *Professor Ukpong,*
         I am sorry that it has taken so long for
         me to contact you and I hope you still check
         this email page. I just cannot thank you enough
         for the prayers that you have given up to the
         Lord on my behalf, in my time of need. If it
         was not for who you are and God putting you
         within my path, I would not have had the will
         to go on and graduate nursing school. You will
         forever be in my heart and my prayers. Thank
         you again for your good work for the Lord and
         may He always shine His light upon you.

(14) I had a nursing student who was doing well academically
     but failed her ATI (Assessment Technology Institute)
     predictor exam in her final semester. She was very dis-
     traught about it, since she did not expect this kind of
     a result. She was not going to be allowed to take her
     NCLEX because she failed the ATI exam. She came to
     me to see if I could help her. By this time, I was already
     retired, so I could not have any input in the decision
     making of the program. I made her aware of my position
     and told her that I would check into the situation for
     her. This took place on Sunday. Monday morning before
     8:00 AM, I went to the college, waiting for the Director
     of Nursing to come in to work. When the Director
     came in, I presented her with the student's concern.
     The Director asked me to tell the student to send in her
     appeal letter. As she turned to her desk, this student's

appeal letter was already there. She told me I could go, since the information was there and the faculty would be holding a meeting to discuss the matter at 11:00 AM. As a result from the meeting, the student was allowed to take her NCLEX and she passed on her first attempt. This made both the student and me ecstatic and very thankful to God!

(15) I believe that blessings are to be shared and to pay it forward. I was looking for a job in one of the local hospitals in Worcester. I needed a 7:15 AM to 3:15 PM shift and I preferred a surgical nursing unit. When I went for the job interview, I explained to the Nurse Recruiter why I wanted these hours. I had two little children and my husband was away. I had to put my children in a day care that opened at 7:00 AM until 5:00 PM to come to work. I told her that I just needed 15 minutes to rush from the day care to work. In response to my request, the Nurse Recruiter said, "I will officially schedule you for 8:00 AM to 4:00 PM; I do not want you to rush too much to get into work to avoid an accident. Whenever you get in to work between 7:00 and 8:00 AM would be okay." As she was saying this to me, I became very emotional, tears running down my face. How could she be this kind and understanding? I was surprised because she could have denied me the job based on the hours I wanted. I thanked her and then asked her why she was so kind to me. Her answer was, "I am a mother of little ones too, I understand the struggle of trying to balance work

and also be there for your children." She also assigned me to a surgical unit. This was a great blessing and I was very grateful to her and to God. Since I had until 5:00 PM to pick my kids up from the daycare, I would punch my time card out at the 8 hours' time limit and then go back to the nursing unit to give extra care to my patients. A shower, backrub, walking my patients, getting them something to eat or drink. I felt that God had blessed me with this extra time; I wanted to share that blessing with my patients. I will never forget this nurse recruiter for her kindness and understanding.

CHAPTER 22

Life Lessons

These are some of the life lessons that helped me along life's journey. I hope some of them will be helpful to you:

(1)   Believe, trust and lean on the Lord Jesus and He will see you through all the twists and turns of life. The Lord did not promise us an easy road in life. He promised to be with us all the way. In good or bad times, He will never fail you.

(2)   Be nice to people. You may not remember the good or bad things you did to others, but those people may never forget you.

(3)   Forgive. The sooner you forgive, the better you feel and can move on with your life. Some of the people you are angry with may not even realize that you are still mad at them.

(4)   How you started out in life may not determine how and where you end up.

(5) If you do not "use it," you "lose it," be it your mind or your muscle.

(6) Hard work pays off. Not doing anything may never change your current situation.

(7) Do not forget where you started from when you get to the top and do not treat the beginners as if they are know-nothings. No one started at the top. Respect everyone; we all have potential if given the opportunity.

(8) Love, appreciate and take good care of yourself. There is only one "You" in the whole world!

(9) There is no easy road to success. This is why not everyone is successful. Winners do not quit and quitters do not win. Learn to keep going when things get tough.

(10) I don't look at failure as failure, I look at failure as an opportunity for God's redirection. Learn and grow from your mistakes and failures, they can open new doors of opportunity for you.

(11) Learning is lifelong; it is not only for "Students." Anyone who thinks he/she knows it all is deceiving himself or herself and no reasonable person would believe them. People that say and act as if they know it all are trying to hide their insecurities. There are always new things to learn.

(12) Having a dream gives you a focal point and a sense of direction in life to be successful.

(13) One step at a time puts uncountable mileage in your life's journey.

(14) Pay it forward. When someone does well for you, pass that goodness to others. This makes the world a better and kinder place to be.

(15) Try not to provoke people because you do not know what they are going through at that moment. Always put yourself in the other person's shoes.

(16) Know what you want and go for it, whatever it takes. This is how your dreams come true.

(17) Have balance in your life. Too much or too little of anything is not good for you.

(18) Do not worry about things that would not help you with your current situation. Worrying about everything at the same time causes confusion and anxiety. "DON'T GO THERE," if it is not helpful to you for now.

CHAPTER 23

Conclusion

have learned to live one day at a time and take one step at a time. By doing this, I concentrate all my attention, energy, and resources on what I have at hand. Yesterday is gone; tomorrow I do not have any control over. This attitude keeps me from worrying over what and where I do not have control. Worrying now about the past and the future drains your mind and energy from the task at hand, increases your stress level and is not helpful. A day at a time has brought me this far in life, when I look back; it is sometimes unbelievable how far I have come.

I am thankful to God that all my dreams came true even more than I had ever expected or imagined. I had sworn the last day I walked out of my brother's house to go to secondary school, that I would maintain my independence for the rest of my life and would raise my children by myself, so that they would not go through what I went through in my childhood. It feels so, so good to have achieved those dreams. I truly appreciate the ending of my life's journey compared to the beginning. I hope sharing my life's story will help anybody who is reading this book in some ways. Instead of giving up when life's ride gets tough, you tighten your seat belt and *ride* it out. This always ends you in a better position than where you started. Besides, the tough ride is always temporary; it will pass if you do not give up. Life sometimes is not obliged to work out the way you thought you wanted it to.

My parents lived to see my progress. My mother was very happy and proud of me for who I became. She had 31 grandchildren and some great grandchildren before she died. Even though I was too far from home to take care of my parents, I took over their care financially until both of them died at a good old age, my dad died first in 1984, then my mom ten years later in 1994. I never spent Christmas again in Nigeria with my family since I left for America in 1969.

I had prayed to stay away from my brother and his wife. The Lord answered that prayer by making it possible for me to come to America. I never again had to deal with them for the rest of my life! This made me happy. I always stopped by to see them very briefly, whenever I visited Nigeria.

Even though it was an arranged marriage, my brother stayed married to his wife until his passing in March 2018. His wife died in January 2019. They had eight children together, four boys, and four girl.

My small village is now a big town, with modern houses, paved roads, electricity and all that you would expect in a developed city. It is unbelievable how much my village has changed today. With electricity all over my village today, people do not even realize when the moon is out, whereas it was a big deal for us then in the early 1950's. I never went back to live there but still visit when I go to Nigeria.

I am happy, thankful, humbled and appreciative of the grace of God that I did not give up against all odds. It paid off in the end. I have been happily married for 39 years, so far. I am a lucky mother of three wonderful grown children, with an awesome daughter-in-law; I have three beautiful grandchildren, and am a well-established healthcare and education professional.

I have resolved to lessen the burdens of others the best I can, whenever I can. God sent many people to guide and direct my path in life, to a great success. He has given me the opportunity to do the same thing for others. It has been extremely rewarding to be used of the Lord to be a blessing to my patients, their families, my students, co-workers, and other people I meet. The Lord has given me the opportunity and the platform to do this in the Nursing Profession. If I were to be called of the Lord any day, I will happily answer that call because I feel my mission has been accomplished by the grace of God. While waiting for that day, I will continue to give my very best in all that I do every day, to the Glory of God.